Indigenous Peoples and Politics

Edited by
Franke Wilmer
Montana State University

A Routledge Series

Indigenous Peoples and Politics
Franke Wilmer, *General Editor*

Inventing Indigenous Knowledge
Archaeology, Rural Development, and the Raised Field Rehabilitation Project in Bolivia
Lynn Swartley

The Globalization of Contentious Politics
The Amazonian Indigenous Rights Movement
Pamela L. Martin

Cultural Intermarriage in Southern Appalachia
Cherokee Elements in Four Selected Novels by Lee Smith
Kateřina Prajnerová

Storied Voices in Native American Texts
Harry Robinson, Thomas King, James Welch, and Leslie Marmon Silko
Blanca Schorcht

On the Streets and in the State House
American Indian and Hispanic Women and Environmental Policymaking in New Mexico
Diane-Michele Prindeville

Chief Joseph, Yellow Wolf, and the Creation of Nez Perce History in the Pacific Northwest
Robert R. McCoy

National Identity and the Conflict at Oka
Native Belonging and Myths of Postcolonial Nationhood in Canada
Amelia Kalant

Native American and Chicano/a Literature of the American Southwest
Intersections of Indigenous Literature
Christina M. Hebebrand

The Present Politics of the Past
Indigenous Legal Activism and Resistance to (Neo)Liberal Governmentality
Seán Patrick Eudaily

The Ecological Native
Indigenous Peoples' Movements and Eco-Governmentality in Colombia
Astrid Ulloa

Spiraling Webs of Relation
Movements Toward an Indigenist Criticism
Joanne R. DiNova

Negotiating Claims
The Emergence of Indigenous Land Claim Negotiation Policies in Australia, Canada, New Zealand, and the United States
Christa Scholtz

Collective Rights of Indigenous Peoples
Identity-Based Movement of Plain Indigenous in Taiwan
Jolan Hsieh

The State and Indigenous Movements
Keri E. Iyall Smith

THE STATE AND INDIGENOUS MOVEMENTS

Keri E. Iyall Smith

Routledge
New York & London

Routledge
Taylor & Francis Group
270 Madison Avenue
New York, NY 10016

Routledge
Taylor & Francis Group
2 Park Square
Milton Park, Abingdon
Oxon OX14 4RN

© 2006 by Taylor & Francis Group, LLC
Routledge is an imprint of Taylor & Francis Group, an Informa business

Printed in the United States of America on acid-free paper
10 9 8 7 6 5 4 3 2 1

International Standard Book Number-10: 0-415-98016-X (Hardcover)
International Standard Book Number-13: 978-0-415-98016-6 (Hardcover)

No part of this book may be reprinted, reproduced, transmitted, or utilized in any form by any electronic, mechanical, or other means, now known or hereafter invented, including photocopying, microfilming, and recording, or in any information storage or retrieval system, without written permission from the publishers.

Trademark Notice: Product or corporate names may be trademarks or registered trademarks, and are used only for identification and explanation without intent to infringe.

Library of Congress Cataloging-in-Publication Data

Iyall-Smith, Keri, date.
  The state and indigenous movements / by Keri E. Iyall Smith.
    p. cm. -- (Indigenous peoples and politics)
  Includes bibliographical references and index.
  ISBN 0-415-98016-X (alk. paper)
  1. Hawaiians--Civil rights. 2. Hawaiians--Ethnic identity. 3. Hawaiians--Government relations. 4. Indigenous peoples--Civil rights. 5. Indigenous peoples--Ethnic identity. 6. Indigenous peoples--Government relations. 7. Self-determination, National. 8. Hybridity (Social sciences) 9. Hawaii--Colonization. 10. Hawaii--Politics and government. I. Title.

DU624.65.L93 2006
305.8--dc22   2006018945

Visit the Taylor & Francis Web site at
http://www.taylorandfrancis.com

and the Routledge Web site at
http://www.routledge-ny.com

To Clarence. Thank you for your thoughtful, encouraging words.

Contents

List of Figures ... ix

Preface ... xi

Acknowledgments ... xiii

Chapter One
Introduction ... 1

Chapter Two
Research Design ... 21

Chapter Three
On Indigenousness ... 33

Chapter Four
The Hawaiians ... 45

Chapter Five
Global, Local, and/or Hybrid Identities ... 67

Chapter Six
New Applications of Human Rights ... 83

Chapter Seven
Conclusion ... 99

Appendix One
Constitutional Amendments 1–10: The Bill of Rights   109

Appendix Two
United States Public Law 103–150   111

Appendix Three
The Constitution of the State of Hawaii: Article XII, Selected Sections   117

Appendix Four
Indian Civil Rights Act of 1968: 25 USC 1302–1303   119

Appendix Five
Universal Declaration of Human Rights, Selected Articles   121

Notes   123

Bibliography   129

Index   145

List of Figures

Figure 3.1.	The Relational Concept: Three Systems	39
Figure 7.1.	The Relational Concept and Identity	102
Figure 7.2.	The Relational Concept and Human Rights	103

Preface

> Virtually all American political theorists treat the United States as a polyethnic nation-state, rather than a truly multination state. Perhaps this is because national minorities in the United States are relatively small and isolated (e.g. Puerto Rico, American Indians, native Hawaiians, Alaskan Eskimos). These groups are virtually invisible in American political theory. If they are mentioned at all, it is usually as an afterthought. This has had a profound effect on liberal thought around the world, since American theorists have become the dominant interpreters of liberal principles since World War II (Kymlicka 1995: 56).

The invisibility of indigenous peoples is a problem in American society and world society. Many indigenous communities—tribes, bands, extended families, or Nations—fall between the cracks at state and international levels. Their size may be great, but invisibility can render indigenous groups powerless. Growing up I saw this happen for the tribe that I am enrolled in, the Cowlitz Tribe. Generations of my family have worked to achieve federal recognition from the United States government, which was finally granted only five years ago.

As a child, my only knowledge of the tribe and my heritage consisted of memories of council meetings in a hot place, a rocky parking lot out front, and a nice lady who used to offer my brother and me food for being quiet while the meetings took place. My father was often dressed up in slacks, and wearing a tie and leather shoes for these meetings. He was the vice-chairman of the tribe. I also recall a long trip to a muddy place in the woods where people talked a lot about things I did not really understand. My father has pictures of his family on the farm on the Nisqually Indian reservation. My great aunt still owns the farm, but it is in disrepair. The local priest used to say a Catholic mass in the family home.

As I began to participate in the American Indian community on campus at the University of Washington, I discovered a strong gatekeeping effort that was wary of my participation and my identity. I have been an official member of the Cowlitz tribe since March 26, 1974. Yet, this aspect of my identity is invisible. People are sometimes curious about the heritage of the surname Iyall. Most assume that my heritage is white, because I have pale skin and medium brown hair. Although my father has the look of a Northwest coast Indian, I did not seem to inherit many of those traits. Learning to establish my own authenticity within the campus community was a part of gaining some understanding about the American Indian experience.

At the time that my participation in the community grew, my interest in scholarship deepened. Many of the participants in the First Nations at UW student organization were also my colleagues in the American Indian Studies classes. This was a time of awakening for me as a scholar and as a person. The scientific study of American Indians allowed me to get closer to a part of my personal history. I studied sociology, American Indians, gaming as a form of economic development on reservations, American Indians and the criminal justice system, and the Federal Acknowledgment Process via the Branch of Acknowledgement Research office. My research implicitly recognized the context: indigenous peoples live as internal colonies.

I arrived at UNC-Chapel Hill hoping to study crime and American Indians, planning to work closely with John Hagan. His quick departure from the department left me running in place as I sought to find a new mentor, and a new direction for my studies. My master's thesis on colonialism and religion's influence on liberal democracy prepared me for a shift to the sociological study of colonialism. This gradually evolved to an exploration of the indigenous experience at the federal and international level. The research project that follows is the beginning of what I hope will be a body of research, considering what it means to be indigenous, exploring in greater depth the experience of being colonized, and seeking additional means of attaining sovereignty for indigenous Nations.

I am coming into my own as a social scientist who happens to be an American Indian. The experiences of myself, my family members, and the Cowlitz tribe have given me a desire to seek space for those who fall in between. I value the voice of the community, have a unique understanding of pluralism, and see the world as one with pockets of exclusion and invisibility. The experience of the Cowlitz tribe is but one example and there are many similar cases around the world. I recognize that there are gaps that allow legitimate indigenous communities to fall through the cracks of State and international rights regimes, and will continue to explore solutions that sociological study can illuminate.

Acknowledgments

I thank Judith R. Blau for her guidance, support, and assistance as I developed and completed this project. Her supervision was both structured and liberating, allowing me to follow and explore the ideas and conditions that were most interesting to me. Thank you to Andrew J. Perrin for reading and commenting on early drafts of the manuscript. I also wish to thank my dissertation committee: Judith R. Blau, William A. Darity, Michael D. Green, Ted Mouw, and Andrew J. Perrin, for encouraging me and for being a part of this project.

Chapter One
Introduction

My interests in the Native Hawaiians started with a trip to the island of Oahu in the summer of 1995. Even as a tourist, I could not avoid the plebiscite headlines in the media. Although the vote had not yet been conducted, it stirred up controversy almost daily. Being a student of Sociology and American Indian Studies, news of the plebiscite caught my attention. This was a contentious issue with high stakes on both sides. For the Native Hawaiians the plebiscite might be a way to attain justice for the illegal overthrow of their kingdom. For the non-indigenous peoples living in Hawai'i, roughly sixty-six percent of the state population, the plebiscite could mean arbitrary deprivation of property and citizenship. The plebiscite, which took place in 1996, was the third plebiscite in Hawaiian history. The first two plebiscites resulted in support of joining the United States (Sluyk 1996). Yet the Apology Bill issued in 1993 recognized that Native Hawaiians had not willfully surrendered their sovereignty to the United States. This Bill forced the third plebiscite, which was framed in a confusing and controversial manner. The Hawaiian Sovereignty Election Committee asked the question: "shall the Hawaiian people elect delegates to propose a Native Hawaiian government?" The Unrepresented Nations and Peoples Organization argues that this was not, in fact, a plebiscite vote (Sluyk 1996). Although yes votes outnumbered no votes in this final plebiscite, the turnout was so low that it was not sufficient to approve the measure. In the meanwhile, under the Akaka Bill the United States government is attempting to "recognize" the Native Hawaiians as a tribe, hoping to skirt the sovereignty issue.

During this same visit, I also saw news reports on "beach people," people who were living on public beaches. Many "beach people" were Native Hawaiians who had been evicted from their homes while awaiting their promised allotment. Others were protesters, seeking to publicize the long waits for Hawaiian Homelands. They were feared as criminals and subject to arrest for trespassing. Property prices are high on an island, especially an island with a strong tourism industry *and* a military outpost. Occupation of the beaches—by the homeless or protesters—was made illegal by the State of Hawaii, the foreign State that built up around the indigenous Hawaiians. I felt sympathy for the indigenous beach people, forced to live in their cars while others benefited from the unlawful usurpation of authority and resources.

While embarking on this is project, I remembered the Native Hawaiians. This book will consider their history and experience closely as a case study. I also examine the Mayans of Mexico. The study of both the Native Hawaiians and Mayans allows me to explore indigenous groups' rights within the contexts of globalization and state oppression. I critically review how the colonial experience, from both internal and external colonial powers, stripped indigenous groups of their identities and their ties to the land. Human rights instruments, I find, will be the best means of restoring rights and freedoms to indigenous Nations.

THE CONTEXT

Globalization is a set of processes resulting in a shrinking of the globe and the spread of the idea that we live in one world. A developing global community is interacting with local communities to change both the global and the local populations. People are moving more than ever, as immigrants, travelers, refugees, and entering countries on student visas or as short-term employees. Communication, travel, and experience are expanding our imaginations. Communication networks move images, words, and money around the world at the speed of light. Commodities are traded worldwide, and increasingly made worldwide. Components are manufactured in various factories and then assembled in another factory. The finished product might be sold locally or abroad. States must work together in unprecedented ways to allow for the standardization this requires.

Political bodies are also globalizing, with the increasing role of regional and international governing bodies. Globalization squeezes and stretches the State, regions, and the international system of States. Borders are becoming more fluid to allow the passing of goods, people, and communiqués. In a globalized society, it is difficult to conceptualize the State independent of the exterior influences (Hall 1997). The State is at a risk of becoming less relevant as multinational corporations and international governing organizations are becoming the dominant actors. Yet the state is also needed to enforce regulations that benefit corporations and global governance, and to protect citizens from corporate interests and overzealous governance.

As globalization spreads, local and global communities are interacting: localisms are becoming universalized and the universal is becoming localized (Robertson 1992). Local communities are fragile: the local is bombarded with outside influences from all sides. The community must work to protect and maintain its locality. The global culture is dynamic. It is centered in the West, speaks English, is a partial homogenization (Hall 1997), and is influenced by the media (Appadurai 1998, Beck 2000). Hybrid identities are also forming, which merge the local and the global elements. These identities are not the product of assimilation, but instead are the result of an agentic process that incorporates elements of the local culture with parts of the global culture.

Within their boundaries, States attempt to create relatively homogenous communities by promoting nationalism and assimilation. Yet, the populations within State borders are not homogeneous. Religious, ethnic, national, and linguistic differences create lines of division. Elements of globalization render "the myth of a culturally homogeneous state even more unrealistic, and has forced the majority within each state to be more open to pluralism and diversity" (Kymlicka 1995: 9). With globalization fostering and encouraging pluralistic expressions of identity and language, an appreciation of diversity and pluralism is spreading to all segments of society.

Indigenous groups' needs exist outside of the boundaries of what the State can provide, and as such they must seek rights from another entity. In this case they seek freedoms from international governing organizations charged with protecting human rights. Yet borders do not hinder indigenous groups' chances. Hybridity allows indigenous groups to traverse boundaries in two ways: it gives them the ability to communicate in the language of the political system and it creates a bridge across the cultural gaps. With hybridity, indigenous groups are able to overcome the threats to their communities wrought by globalization. They are able to use the tools provided by globalization to protect *and* grow their local communities.

INDIGENOUS

Names of indigenous tribes in the United States often mean "the people" in the local language. Cosmologies often describe journeys to the land they now call home. Tribes in the Americas, Asia, Australia, and other areas are *"indigenous* because their ancestral roots are imbedded in the lands in which they live, or would like to live, much more deeply than the roots of more powerful sectors of society living on the same lands or in close proximity" (Anaya 1996: 3). For indigenous Nations, land's value lies not in its economic potential, but as a cultural home. The land is a part of the community. Resources of the land are used by indigenous Nations, but not pillaged.

Combining definitions, I define indigenous[1] as living descendants of the pre-contact (generally contact by Europeans) aboriginal inhabitants (United Nations Working Group on Indigenous Populations 1994; Anaya 1996) who were living in tradition-based autonomous communities (Guibernau 1999). Indigenous Nations are culturally distinct (Anaya 1996, Guibernau 1999), and often live as internal colonies, "engulfed by settler societies born of the forces of empire and conquest" (Anaya 1996:3; United Nations Working Group on Indigenous Populations 1994). In the present day, indigenous Nations have incorporated elements of the outside society, while remaining rooted in local traditions (United Nations Working Group on Indigenous Populations 1994). The application of indigenous as it is defined here can be broad, to include European ethnic groups (such as the Basques, Irish, or Welsh) in addition to New World indigenous Nations (such as the Native Hawaiians, American Indians, or First Nations of Canada).

Indigenous groups fall into many different categories of types of groups. They are internal colonies, Nations without a State, and oppressed peoples. Each implies something different. As internal colonies and oppressed peoples, indigenous communities are defined in opposition to another body and not from within. Indigenous groups are also one type of Nation, linking ethnicity and group membership with cultural cohesion. Many American Indian tribes have long referred to themselves as Nations and are described as such in treaties. Other indigenous groups use this term to describe their communities. Thus, I refer to indigenous communities as indigenous Nations throughout this book.

AMERICAN INDIANS AND NATIVE HAWAIIANS CONTRASTED

American Indians and Native Hawaiians, although seemingly similar, are very different due to the legal history of both cases and timing. Unlike American Indians,[2] the Native Hawaiians do not have a treaty relationship with the federal government. Native Hawaiians do not have a government-to-government relationship with the United States Federal Government. To further establish the distinction between Native

Hawaiians and American Indians, I describe the tribal relationship with the federal government, the Native Hawaiians' relationship with the federal government, and then present three examples. The first example examines the Federal Indian Law textbook, the second looks at a lawsuit, and the third looks at the text of a law protecting indigenous peoples' graves. In each case, the American Indians and Native Hawaiians are implicitly or explicitly presented as being distinct from each other.

Indian tribes' relationship with the federal government is defined as a treaty relationship (Deloria and Wilkins 1999). American Indian sovereignty is tied to tribal bodies and their treaties. Under Federal Indian law, sovereignty is defined as tribal sovereignty (Canby 1988). Congress is free to extinguish tribal sovereignty at any time by abrogating treaties. In addition to this, the plenary power of congress allows for the passage of laws that limit tribal sovereignty. Tribal sovereignty is not absolute, but "exists entirely at the sufferance of Congress" (Canby 1988:79). Compared to American Indians, Native Hawaiians have a different status and experience.

The United States has a long history of influence in the Hawaiian Kingdom, but it was only when Hawai'i joined the union—first as a territory and then as a state—that the federal government was formally responsible for the protection of the Native Hawaiian people. Hawai'i came under United States jurisdiction via a hostile taking of the land and sovereignty. The rights of Native Hawaiians were terminated upon the takeover by the United States when it annexed the Hawaiian territory. No treaties were negotiated. The State of Hawai'i made allowances for Native Hawaiians at the request of the federal government, but the federal government did not negotiate directly with the Native Hawaiians to create the Office of Hawaiian Affairs. Specifically, the text of the Act admitting Hawai'i to the union required the State of Hawai'i to hold the trust lands and the income from the lands (Getches, Wilkinson and Williams 1993). The United States government charged the State of Hawai'i with creating protections of Native Hawaiians, making this a requirement for the attainment of statehood.

Federal Indian Law generally applies only to American Indians living in the continental United States. The casebook on American Indian Law (Getches, Wilkinson, and Williams 1993) sets the rights of Alaskan Natives and Native Hawaiians apart from Indian Law in the final section of the textbook that covers these two topics and international legal perspectives on indigenous rights. This implicitly likens Alaskan Natives and Native Hawaiians to international indigenous groups. The casebook is over one thousand pages long, yet it includes only thirty pages on the Native Hawaiians. The small amount of space (roughly three percent) dedicated to law pertaining to Native Hawaiians is indicative of the role of Native Hawaiians in Federal Legal cases.

In the proceedings of Price v. State of Hawai'i (764 F.2d), it is clear that Native Hawaiians fall through the jurisdictional cracks. In this case a community that calls itself the Hou Hawaiians, a subgroup or tribe of the Native Hawaiians, is seeking the right to sue the state on the grounds that it breached its trust obligations. They allege that the state has failed to expend trust funds for the betterment of Native Hawaiians, as it is supposed to under the Constitution of the State of Hawai'i (as stated in section 5(f) of the Hawaiian Homes Commission). The Hou assert the right to sue under § 1362 Jurisdiction and § 1331 Jurisdiction, but both are rejected. Section 1362 jurisdiction applies to an Indian tribe or band recognized by the Secretary of the Interior (Price v. State of Hawai'i: 1985). Section 1331 jurisdiction applies to rights or immunities created by the Constitution or law of the Untied States (Price v. State of Hawai'i: 1985). The court finds that the Hou are not an Indian tribe or band recognized by the Secretary of the Interior, and the court finds that the enforcement of §5(f) is a federal question (Price v. State of Hawai'i: 1985). Although it seems that the Hou have a win for making their claim under § 1331 Jurisdiction, because they cannot claim an implied private cause of action, they cannot sue the State of Hawai'i (Price v. State of Hawai'i: 1985). The Hou cannot claim a private cause of action by law, because the United States is not a formal trustee of the § 5(f) homelands trust (Price v. State of Hawai'i: 1985). The court proceedings further indicate that individual Hawaiians do not have an implied cause of action under the Admission Act (Price v. State of Hawai'i: 1985). This puts the Hou in a double bind: they cannot assert their rights as a collective because they are not recognized as such, and they cannot individually assert their rights because the law does not allow it. Further, this case excludes Native Hawaiians from rights due to federally recognized tribes, implicitly excluding Native Hawaiians from Federal Indian law.

Another example of how American Indians and Native Hawaiians differ can be found in the Definitions section of the Native American Graves Protection and Repatriation Act (NAGPRA) (U.S. Congress, House 1990). Among the fifteen numbered definitions are Indian tribe, Native American, Native Hawaiian, Native Hawaiian organization, and Office of Hawaiian Affairs. Note that Indian, Native American, and Native Hawaiian are explicitly treated separately. The definition of the term "tribal land" is subdivided into three sections: lands within the boundaries of any Indian reservation, dependent Indian Communities, and lands administered for the benefit of Native Hawaiians under the Hawaiian Homes Commission Act (U.S. Congress, House 1990). The landholdings are also different legally, as illustrated by the sub-sections that define tribal land. By separating the Native Hawaiians, the law affirms the "different" status of Native Hawaiians as compared to American Indians. Reading through the text of the act, the Native Hawaiians continue to be discussed as a separate entity from Indian tribes. Alaskan natives are not distinguished in the same manner. This is illustrative of how federal law relates to and defines Native Hawaiians and American Indians.

Hawai'i negotiated treaties with the United States before it became a territory. Yet, Native Hawaiians have no treaty relationship with the government. The treaty era of Federal Indian Law ended in 1815, although some legal scholars are calling for a renewal of the treaty relationship between tribes and the United States government (Deloria and Wilkins 1999). The Native Hawaiians may not be included in this shift, as they have not had a history of a treaty relationship with the United States. American Indians and Native Hawaiians are very different in terms of their legal status in United States federal law. Yet, both groups experience a similar social, economic, and political status within the United States and in the various localities. American Indian groups (e.g. tribes, bands, or Nations) and Native Hawaiians are internal colonies and share the same challenges of overcoming the experience of being colonized. Unlike many American Indian tribes that were able to negotiate with the American government, Native Hawaiians were denied this right. Their sovereignty was taken by force.

A POLITICAL MOVEMENT

Political movements attempt to assert a competing ideology. Here I will consider three types of movements identified and described by theorists: old social movements, new social movements, and anti-systemic movements. Old social movements include the "labor movement, with its organized trade unions and political parties, which was taken to be the norm" (Nash 2000:125). The new social movement is considered new because it is not a labor or socialist movement, like the classic old social movement (Calhoun 2000 [1993]). New social movements make limited, non-negotiable demands; politicize everyday life; do not mobilize along class lines; are organized in non-hierarchical and democratic ways; engage in novel political tactics; and are not united by one over-arching organization (Nash 2000). Anti-systemic movements work outside the world-system, seeking significant changes to the capitalist world-system.

Indigenous nationalist movements do not exemplify old social movements. Indigenous Nations are not political parties or organizations protecting the rights of laborers. Their shared sentiments and goals are not about achieving class-related gains. Movement participants are not union members seeking higher wages, a safer work environment, health insurance benefits, or class based gains. The indigenous nationalist movement is about achieving some form of political independence from the State, which is different from the shape and purpose of the old social movement.

Indigenous movements can be viewed, to some extent, as new social movements. Defining features of new social movements include: focus on identity, autonomy, and self-realization; are defensive instead of offensive; politicize everyday life; are not mobilized along class lines; forms and style of movement actions exemplify the values of the movement; employ unconventional means; and have partial and overlapping commitments to other movements (Calhoun 2000 [1993]). These movements often include many, if not all, of the defining features of new social movements. Indigenous nationalist movements are distinct in that they are seeking change within the political system, but they are also seeking to create new political systems. They are internal colonies that are seeking freedom from the colonial powers. Because of these elements, the indigenous nationalist movement is a distinct form of social movement, and cannot be categorized as a new or old social movement.

Indigenous nationalist movements are also seeking to change international norms. Norms are very powerful, with the ability to "channel and regularize behavior; they often limit the range of choice and constrain actions" (Finnemore and Sikkink 1998:894). The norm life cycle includes norm emergence, norm acceptance, and norm internationalization (Finnemore and Sikkink 1998). The termination of the life cycle is not inevitable. Global norms are constantly being made and remade (Brown Thompson 2002). Thus, the termination of the United Nations Trusteeship Council in 1994 suggests that decolonization is complete. This norm, decolonization, has been so successfully adopted that there is no need for the Trusteeship Council to remain in existence. Yet, the emergence of the United Nations Working Group on Indigenous Peoples might signal a new norm emerging, the norm of self-determination. As decolonization appears to be at the end of its norm life cycle, a new norm is in the phase of emergence. Transnational actors can contribute to norm formation (Brown Thompson 2002), initiate a process of norm shift (Sikkink 2002), and teach new norms (Khagram, Riker, and Sikkink 2002). Via political movements, indigenous Nations are seeking to promote the emergence of a norm of self-determination. Locally and globally, indigenous Nations shame the State that limits their sovereignty. They internationalize domestic disputes by making appeals to organizations such as the United Nations and the Unrepresented Peoples and Nations Organization.

Indigenous Nations might be inverting Finnemore and Sikkink's life cycle, using norm internationalization to achieve norm acceptance. This process of reshaping international norms can bring change to the indigenous experience locally and globally, and it might also reshape the world-system.

Indigenous movements embody anti-systemic movements in an age of transition. Looking at the many movement organizations seeking change within the Native Hawaiian movement, it is possible to find all of the four strategic considerations: open debate about the transition and outcome, short-term defensive action, establishment of middle-range goals, and the development of substantive meaning of long term goals (Wallerstein 2002). For indigenous Nations, the collective is often more important than the individual. Maximizing economic gains is not the most important goal. Family, community, and culture are priorities instead. Indigenous groups will never fully integrate with the world-system as it exists today and they are actively engaged in the transition.

WORLD-SYSTEMS THEORY

World-systems analysis is a method of study with a specific unit of analysis: the world-system, which is an historical social system that encompasses the entire globe (Wallerstein 2000). World-systems research is historic and systemic. Capitalism is the economy of the world-system. In the world-system there are three structural positions: core, periphery, and semi-periphery. Anti-systemic movements are working within the State and international systems while attempting to shape an alternate framework for attaining political power both within the State and internationally (Wallerstein 2000). The world-system is currently in a structural crisis, and is moving into a period of transition (Wallerstein 2002). It is unknown what form the new system will take.

NATION

The word Nation has its root in the Latin term meaning birth. The French Revolution is often cited as the beginning of the Nation. In other sources the American Revolution is the first example of a Nation. Both are early Nations. Research and theory of the Nation are extensive. The definitions vary widely, in general including cultural elements while minimizing political or bureaucratic components.

While Connor (1994 [1978]) regards the Nation as intangible, something that can only be self-defined, Geertz (1994 [1963]) identifies several defining characteristics of a Nation: blood ties, race, language, region, religion, and custom. These two represent the most and least demanding definitions. There are many definitions in between. Renan (1994 [1882]) says a Nation consists of two things: a common legacy of remembrances and the desire to live together and value the common heritage. For Deutsch (1994 [1966]), nationalities (a group that is able to communicate more easily within the community than with outsiders) become Nations when they have the power to back up their aspirations. Generally these definitions share elements of intangible and communal ties. They are less explicit.

Other definitions of the Nation require more concrete indicators. Oommen (1997) says there are only two elements needed to be a Nation: common territory and common language. Hechter and Borland's (2001) definition of the Nation includes common heritage, distinct culture, and spatial concentration. Stalin (1994 [1973]) says a Nation has: a stable historically constituted community, a common language, a common territory, common economic life, and a common psychological make-up. For Guibernau (1999) a Nation is a community with consciousness that shares culture, defined territory, a common past and goals for the future. The Nation claims the right to self-rule (Guibernau 1999). The definition penned by Kymlicka (1995) indicates that a Nation is a historical community sharing a distinct territory or homeland, language, and culture.

In his writing debunking other concepts included in definitions of the Nation, Weber (1946) suggests that many concepts are insufficient and unnecessary: a common language, blood ties, citizenship, a common anthropological type (e.g. race), and ethnic solidarity. Thus, he concludes, "a nation is a community which normally tends to produce a state of its own" (Weber 1946: 176). This is a parsimonious and demanding definition. It includes scope, allows the community to define itself, and implies but does not demand bureaucratic structure.

To define the Nation it is essential to avoid confusion with ethnicity, race, or the State. Nations may share language, race, culture, history, economic life, or a desire to live together. But what distinguishes a Nation is Weber's definition: a community that normally tends to produce a State of its own. I would like to qualify Weber's definition, adding that the community might also tend to seek greater governing power within a State[3] that stops short of actual statehood. In addition to this change, a common relationship to territory should be added as a necessary but not sufficient condition to defining the Nation. This amends the requirements of common territory found in definitions by Stalin (1994 [1973]), Kymlicka (1995), Oommen (1997), Guibernau (1999), and Hechter and

Introduction 11

Borland (2001). A common relationship to territory can be expressed as rootless (e.g. nomads), a familial link, or it may take on another form.

STATE

International political systems revolve around the State as a political body. Aristotle, Hobbes, Rousseau, and others describe the bureaucratic and legislative aspect of the State, citing its role in enforcing and regulating social contracts. The State is a compound of citizens (Aristotle 1968). Yet, States are made up of a diverse citizenry. It is impossible to form a State for each national or cultural community: cultures are not discrete and the number of national groups is too large (Tully 1995). The constitution of the State is essential in defining the State further: both its character and its role as a political body. States exist to enforce social contracts (Hobbes 1962) and States have the power to regulate (Hobbes 1962; Weber 1978). The State seeks to standardize transactions within its boundaries, rejecting métis in favor of uniform, State-sanctioned canon (Scott 1998). The State is charged with the task of carrying out the will of the people (Rousseau 1968). To this end, the State enforces rights and rules (Levi 1988).

Emphasizing the enforcement arm of the State, the State has binding authority over actions within its boundaries (Weber 1978). The State has a monopoly on the legitimate use of physical force within established boundaries (Weber 1946). Skocpol echoes this sentiment (1998), saying the State must be able to maintain order. All constitutional States are equal in authority (Tully 1995). Wallerstein (1997b) identifies two types of State sovereignty: inward and outward. Inward sovereignty refers to a State's ability to freely create policies within its boundaries and outward sovereignty prohibits others States from exerting authority within its boundaries (Wallerstein 1997b). No State is truly sovereign in either sense (Wallerstein 1997b), yet the maintenance of this idea supports the capitalist world-system and the State's dominance in the international community.

The State's relation to territory is another aspect of the definition. "What characterizes a State is territorially bounded and centralized regulation of important aspects of social life" (Levi 1988:1). The State has a territorial basis (Weber 1978). Oommen places territory at the core of his definition of the State: "an entity that is endowed with political sovereignty over a clearly defined territorial area" (Oommen 1997:23). The State is a bordered power-container (Giddens 1994 [1985]). For the State, territory is an economic resource to be exploited. The land has use value for farming, mining, and is a commodity. Even cultural sites hold economic value as tourist sites.

The State is a regulatory and enforcement body with a territorial base. A State has sovereignty over a defined territory (Evans, Rueschemeyer and Skocpol 1985; Levi 1988; Giddens 1994 [1985]; and Oommen 1997). State sovereignty includes a monopoly on the legitimate use of violence (Weber 1946 and Weber 1978) and the regulation and enforcement of social contracts (Hobbes 1962; Rousseau 1968; Evans, Rueschemeyer and Skocpol's 1985). The State is also an autonomous actor (Skocpol 1998). Finally, the system of States is not unchangeable (Tully 1995). These elements best describe a State's political and bureaucratic power along with the basis and boundaries of the power.

NATION-STATE

The nation-state is a distinct entity that exists when one Nation has its own State (Connor 1994 [1978]). Nation-state implies a homogenous population, sharing one national identity (Deutsch 1994 [1966]; Oommen 1997). The hyphenated term was created for a reason: "to describe a territorial-political unit (a state) whose borders coincided or nearly coincided with the territorial distribution of a national group" (Connor 1994 [1978]:39).[4] Nation-state projects in France, Great Britain, Germany, Turkey, Indonesia, Philippines, Rwanda, Burundi, and Nigeria are failures at creating a single national identity within the populace of the State (Oommen 1997). These bodies are States and multi-national States, but not nation-states. It is essential to re-introduce the more precise meaning of nation-state, and use it with care to avoid confusing the State with the nation-state.

The nation-state exists in rare circumstances empirically (Connor 1994 [1978]). The majority of the States are multi-national, poly-ethnic, or both (Oommen 1997). It is essential to take care in the use of the term nation-state, not using this term as a synonym of the State. It has been said "traditional political sociology takes the modern nation-state as the center of political activity" (Nash 2000:x). I do not agree with this positioning of the nation-state, and deliberately push it to the background. The nation-state is a minority in the global polity, and the high degree of pluralism that characterizes the globalized world will make this term less relevant.

RELATION BETWEEN THE STATE AND NATION

The State is part of a system of competing and mutually involved States (Evans, Rueschemeyer, and Skocpol 1985). The population of states is relatively small, at one hundred and ninety-two. This is especially small when compared to the number of ethnic or communal groups, estimated at four thousand. States currently have the power, as Lukes (1974) identifies, the power to make change and set the agenda. Yet a large number of ethnic and cultural groups challenge the State at both the local and international levels. As these groups begin to gain entry into international governing organizations such as the European Union and the United Nations, they will only challenge the State and the system of States further.

The setting that the State exists within is changing, weakening and strengthening different aspects of the governing body. International businesses are growing larger in scope and budget than some States. The State relies upon these organizations for economic viability and stability. With the power of multi-national organizations (corporate and political), the State is not as important as it once was. Empirical evidence suggests that State sovereignty is not more threatened due to globalization (Krasner 1999). Yet its permanence is not assured. With globalization, many of the state's functions are becoming obsolete. Yet, citizens need a strong state more than ever, to protect and insulate them from the risks presented by globalization. Indigenous Nations living as internal colonies are seeking to attain rights for their communities within the State, or carve new political territories out of existing States. They need autonomy for cultural, economic, and political survival. Indigenous groups threaten the State in three ways: they pose risk of instability, secession, and border changes.

Indigenous groups threaten local and global political stability. Self-determination can bring changes to international boundaries, the State's role in the international system, and the international State system. These changes are not always welcome. For example, East Timor voted for independence in 1999 and faced resistance from Indonesia as a direct result of the vote. Peacekeepers were needed to protect the East Timorese from the violent response of the Indonesians. State stability was threatened by the East Timorese vote and in the aftermath of the response to the vote. The economy was also threatened by the unrest. The potential shift in boundaries resulting from the East Timor independence vote had both a local and global impact. When a group is able to cut itself away from the larger body, the State loses symbolic strength, political and economic stability, and global stability. This can be a significant loss.

In seeking greater freedoms, indigenous Nations are calling for a division between their group and the existing State. This act is a form of secession, even if the outcome is not a new State. Hobbes' idea that secession is illegitimate is the one that dominates contemporary political theory (Livingston 1998). Yet others advocate a reframing of secession, which can create the space to solve conflicts (Livingston 1998) or become a solution to eroding political liberalism (Hoppe 1996). For liberal democracies to be truly democratic, the door to secession must be open. Indigenous Nations generally seek self-determination or self-government in one of four forms: total sovereignty in the form of a new State; limited sovereignty over a land base—the land base is administered by the indigenous but they remain State citizens; legally incorporated land based units united by a common electoral council; or the Nation within a Nation model (Trask, H. 1999). Thus, self-determination calls for the implementation of either: new territorial boundaries, new political boundaries, or new ideological boundaries. Any of these models can threaten the sovereignty of the State and could be labeled as secession.

State boundaries demand strength, definition, and a degree of permanence for the maintenance of sovereignty. Indigenous communities are finding ways to reassert themselves, maneuvering for more rights and self-determination. The result is a shift in State boundaries. In the case of Hawai'i, a border change puts United States interests at risk. The loss of lands that are agriculturally lucrative, with rich aquatic resources, strategically positioned military bases, and income from the tourism industry would be costly. A shift in State borders would cause the United States to lose land, military positioning, and natural resources. This can weaken the State and threaten its interests.

In the existing global political structure, local communities cannot exist independent of the State context. Instead, indigenous Nations are finding ways to reassert themselves, maneuvering for more rights and self-determination. They might team up with non-government organizations, other indigenous Nations, or international governing organizations, taking advantage of improved technologies and communication. Indigenous nationalist sentiment threatens the State: they endanger local stability, are a form of secession, and risk the integrity of State borders. Indigenous groups, as Nations, benefit by threatening the State.

TERRITORY

Territory has long been important to political bodies, where "the land of empires was known by its power centers and expansiveness, the land of the state was known by its boundaries" (Mukerji 1997:3). Political units use different arguments to extend borders: linguistic similarity, or the presence of a physical boundary (Poggi 1978). State building was in a lull during the aftermath of World War I, when colonial and territorial holdings by external powers increased. Land served as a teaching tool under colonial rule: "the measurement and classification of land was the training ground for the culture of number" (Appadurai 1998: 125). The desire to measure land meticulously, including topography, shows the importance of land and its use (Mukerji 1997). The end of World War II signaled a large abolishment of colonial relationships and another era of State formation. As international political organizations—without territorial boundaries—are growing in importance and ability to enforce a growing body of international law, territorial boundaries remain important for the State.

There is political power attached to territory: it is the base of power and the container for the State. Territorial boundaries establish the boundaries of State sovereignty. The government oversees relations that take place on its soil: political power is attached to boundaries and the territory within. It has a monopoly on the legal use of violence. The State with a capitalist base regulates the economy within its boundaries and the relations across borders, establishing rules for trade and commerce. The State uses the resources of the land to further its political and economic interests. The capitalist State will attempt to maximize the use value of the territory, confiscating the surface and all resources to strengthen the economy and the State. Land is a source of power for the State: as it defines itself, and by enabling the State to have a strong economy.

For the indigenous, land has spiritual and symbolic meaning: it is the root of their community, and sometimes a member of the community. In the cosmology of Native Hawaiians, the land is an ancestor who gave birth to Hawaiians (Trask, H. 1999). Thus, the relationship to the land is a form of kinship. There is a sense of stewardship and of duty to not only use the resources that the land gives for sustenance, but to do what each generation can to perpetuate the health and fertility of the land. Nations place importance on boundaries, yet access is also important. Legal cases regarding access to water and other natural resources are a part of the body of Federal Indian Law in the United States. The Boldt Decision allowing American Indians to enter private property in order to harvest clams in the usual and accustomed places[5] is one example of how rights to access can meet the needs of indigenous Nations. Land has value for its spiritual importance and the resources it yields.

Territory and the construction of unique historical roots empower and authenticate both States and Nations. Community and territory interact to create a sense of place that is important to many groups, cultures, and individuals. The homeland is invented, yet the status of the territory can have real consequences (Anderson 1992). For States, territory defines the physical boundaries and is an economic resource. There are important symbolic and tangible powers given to the State that governs its own territory: Nations without States lack these powers. For Nations territory holds symbolic, sometimes familial, and religious meaning. Territory shapes group identity and difference, because groups are defined as Nations in part by their relation to territory (Oommen 1998). States and Nations have different types of claims to the physical boundaries and the resources within. Indigenous Nations without political power watch as the meaning of land shifts to match the will of the outsiders. Territory can become politicized when there are disputes over the right of access to sites, the use and management of the land, or the power to govern the territory.

HUMAN RIGHTS

There is a body of literature on the study of human rights in international studies, government and policy research. Thus far the sociological contribution to this literature has been minimal. Recently social scientists have begun to examine human rights (Howard and Donnelly 1986; Mitchell, Howard, and Donnelly 1987; and Howard 1995). Human rights encompass the right to what is minimally necessary to live, (Howard 1995) and protect human agency (Ignatieff 2001). The empirical definition of human rights—what is minimally necessary to live, protects agency and agents—are socially constructed. Thus, the empirical expression of human rights is not static, but shifts as the socially defined meaning changes.

Human rights can be divided into three generations of doctrine and enforcement. In first generation human rights, the individual is protected from the State, as exemplified by the United States constitution. The second generation of human rights asserts universal individual rights, beginning with the United Nations' Universal Declaration of Human Rights. The third generation of human rights protects group rights, as exemplified by recent protections of language and culture in United Nations Educational, Scientific and Cultural Organization (UNESCO) doctrine. The application of human rights to collectives is a shift in how human rights are defined, understood, and applied. Yet, in the end individuals will still be the ones to exercise the human rights, as they are the ones who choose to join and participate in collective organizations (here Nations).

This book considers questions about how human rights are defined and how communities are challenging the current definitions. I examine how the meaning of human rights evolves over time by looking at multiple rights granting documents from various time points. Using the cases of Native Hawaiians and the Zapatistas, I consider how the claims of indigenous Nations are stretching the boundaries of human rights doctrine and the enforcement of human rights. The legal community, especially Robert T. Coulter of the Indian Law Resource Center, identifies indigenous rights in terms of human rights. Bringing the study of human rights under

Introduction

a sociological microscope is new. Empirical study of how international human rights are operationalized and challenged in a globalizing society will contribute to the understanding of the construction and enforcement of human rights doctrine.

DESCRIPTION OF THE PROJECT

Indigenous Nations share the experience of being colonized—and the oppression that this entails. This project explores one central research question: what are opportunities for indigenous groups to attain greater rights? I use the Native Hawaiians as a case to make analytical contributions to the study of indigenous groups around the world. To further illustrate the indigenous experience, I also briefly consider the indigenous Mayan groups in Mexico. This is a unique project in sociology. Instead of referring to groups as American Indian, Native American, or Indian, all of which are misnomers, I group all indigenous peoples as one while recognizing the pluralism within the group of indigenous Nations. The use of the term indigenous is deliberate. Not only does it convey the colonial experience in history, but it also applies to the present experience of many indigenous peoples as internal colonies.

This first of seven chapters is about concepts. The second chapter, "Research Design," discusses the methodology, theoretical goals of the project, and the data gathering process. This chapter also includes an explanation of how Native Hawaiians are an illustrative example of indigenousness. In the third chapter, "On Indigenousness," I create a new definition of indigenous and compare it to the traditional definitions. I then problematize indigenousness, describe indigenousness as a relational concept, and consider the label "indigenous" as a means of legitimation. The fourth chapter, "The Hawaiians," introduces the case of the Native Hawaiians. This chapter starts with background information on the condition of Hawaiians at the time of contact, as a United States territory, and up to the present day. I describe the meaning of land to the Hawaiian Nation and then present information on the Hawaiian Renaissance and sovereignty movement organizations.

With the fifth chapter I begin to explore openings for indigenous Nations in the globalizing society. "Global, Local, and/or Hybrid Identities" opens by discussing internal colonialism and globalization to contextualize the conversation. Then, I define and present examples of particular, universal, and hybrid identities. The merging of local and global culture can result in new hybrid cultures. Examples from the Native Hawaiian Nation illustrate the three types of collective identity. I briefly consider the hybrid identity in interactions with the State. The advantages of an early hybrid experience are considered in the conclusion.

In the sixth chapter, "New Applications of Human Rights," I look at how indigenous Nations are transforming consciousness by inserting themselves into the global realm of rights and autonomy. This is another space for opportunity for indigenous Nations. Through their protests against the States that they live within—often as internal colonies—indigenous Nations are bringing new questions about how human rights are conceptualized. Indigenous Nations are appealing to international bodies for the right to assert their identities, as the State system cannot adequately grant these freedoms and protections. This is bringing change to the State, indigenousness, the global moral compass, and conscience.

Finally, the seventh chapter reviews the project. I begin by revisiting the central problem and research question. This is followed by a summary of what the project does, the methodology employed, and the findings. Finally, I re-examine the contributions to the sociological literature and to the interdisciplinary understanding of human rights, political sociology, and world-systems theory. This chapter brings the project full-circle, allowing the reader to synthesize the work and its contributions.

IN SUMMARY

Human rights, the role of territory, and world-systems theory are important concepts that need elaboration in the field of sociology. Applying the sociological imagination to the study of human rights can aid in understanding its construction and operationalization. The study of human rights in sociology is becoming more essential, as this is one way that groups are negotiating to create and maintain State and international norms of behavior. Sociological study of political movements and communities often takes territory for granted. Territory, for indigenous peoples, is essential spiritually *and* for the continuation of culture and life ways. Subsistence living demands access to natural resources. Indigenous Nations seek the right to revere, use, and manage resources as they see fit. This is important for the maintenance of the environment and it is essential for the maintenance of self-determination. Integrating the study of territory expands how political sociology is conceptualized, and allows political sociology to better reflect the politics of the globe. This might also contribute to the sociological understanding of community and the allocation of resources within a community. Ideas for a new socio-economic model might emerge from the sociological study of territory. Finally, this project adds to the literature on world-systems theory with analysis of an anti-systemic movement seeking self-determination—not on the terms of the capitalist world-system, but on its own terms.

Historically, there is little work in the study of indigenous peoples in the field of sociology. Yet, the tide on sociological research that studies indigenous peoples may be shifting. Joanne Nagel (1996) looks at American Indian identity, and literatures on social movements have looked at the American Indian Movement (i.e. Cornell 1988). Other studies of indigenous peoples are demographic (Sandefur, Rindfus, and Cohen 1996 and Snipp 1989), or consider social problems in indigenous populations (crime, alcohol abuse, drugs). At the annual American Sociological Association meetings, paper sessions dedicated to the study of indigenous peoples are telling of future research in this subject area and its role in the discipline. Indigenous Nations are entering the global cultural, political, and economic marketplace. The contribution from sociologists to the literature on indigenous Nations will offer new ideas for debate and analytical research. Sociologists must consider these communities in greater depth, analyzing how their actions may impact the rights and obligations of all members of the international community.

Chapter Two
Research Design

This project's roots are in the identification of inconsistencies and paradoxes. These lead to a research question, what are opportunities for indigenous groups to attain greater rights? With this book I embark on a theoretical exploration of this question with illustrative examples and one case study, the Native Hawaiians. I explore opportunities for indigenous peoples to attain greater rights via the adoption of hybrid identities or under the legal doctrine of international human rights. To be able to talk about these issues sociologically, I must first identify and examine some central terms. In this chapter I present the theoretical goals of this book, briefly introduce the central terms, and describe the methodology employed. I also explain the process of data gathering and offer an account of how Native Hawaiians are an example of indigenousness.

THEORY

Sociology seeks to define society, social interactions, and relationships. The goal of social theory is to describe relationships that are unique to groups. Theoretical work consists of four components: concepts, variables, statements, and formats (Turner 1998). An empirical system must: be plausible (e.g. apply to the real world), satisfy criterion of demarcation, and theory must make a unique contribution to the existing literature (Popper 1959). Social theory can make a contribution to our understanding of society as a whole. Social theory can explain the relationships between groups in society across time, space, and culture.

In the culture of sociology, the study of social reality considers: social groups that have explicable, rational structures exist; within these groups there are subgroups in conflict with each other; and mechanisms of legitimacy contain the conflict (Wallerstein 1999). This project examines the

Native Hawaiians, an example of indigenousness. The Native Hawaiians are a group with rational structures, conflict within the collective, and mechanisms of legitimacy to contain the conflict. Indigenous Nations, more generally, exemplify groups with inner conflict that is managed by mechanisms of legitimation. This project is a theoretical examination of indigenousness. I consider this case "'from the outside,' as a unit of action in the international field," (Zapf 1968:269) following the tradition of the theorizing of imperialism, conquest, and culture contact. Below I introduce multiple theoretical concepts and an interpretation of indigenous as a relational concept in three systems. In later chapters I examine the hybrid identity and human rights doctrine to discover whether or not these things can assist in affording indigenous Nations greater rights and freedoms.

Theoretical Concepts

Theoretical concepts communicate precisely, matter empirically, and generate knowledge claims (Cohen 1989). There are a handful of concepts in this project, including: State, Nation, nation-state, internal colony, indigenous, globalization, global identity, local identity, hybridity, and human rights. Below I concisely define the central concepts. Each is discussed in greater detail within chapters of the book.

- The State is a regulatory body and an enforcement body (Hobbes 1962; Rousseau 1968; Evans, Rueschemeyer and Skocpol's 1985). A State has sovereignty over a defined territory (Evans, Rueschemeyer and Skocpol 1985; Levi 1988; Giddens 1994 [1985]; and Oommen 1997) and a monopoly on the legitimate use of violence (Weber 1946 and Weber 1978). The State is an autonomous actor (Skocpol 1998).

- Nations may share language, race, culture, history, economic life, or a desire to live together. A Nation is a community that tends to produce a State of its own (Weber 1946). The community might also tend to seek greater governing power within a State that stops short of actual statehood. The Nation has a common relationship to territory, which can be expressed as rootless (e.g. nomads), a familial link, or it may take on another form.

- The nation-state is a distinct entity that exists when one Nation has its own State (Connor 1994 [1978]). Nation-state implies a homogenous population, sharing one national identity (Deutsch

1994 [1966]; Oommen 1997). The nation-state exists in rare circumstances empirically (Connor 1994 [1978]). The majority of the States are multi-national, poly-ethnic, or both (Oommen 1997).

- An internal colony is a colony within the boundaries of the State that colonized it. The internal colony is subjected to oppression from the outside government, questions of legitimacy, and forced assimilation. Many American Indian Nations have been colonized more than once, initially by European powers (e.g. Great Britain, France, Spain), and now are internal colonies of the United States.

- Indigenous peoples are descendants of the aboriginal inhabitants (United Nations Working Group on Indigenous Populations 1994; Anaya 1996) who were living in tradition-based autonomous communities (Guibernau 1999). Indigenous Nations are culturally distinct (Anaya 1996, Guibernau 1999) and often live as internal colonies (Anaya 1996; and United Nations Working Group on Indigenous Populations 1994). Indigenous Nations have incorporated elements of the outside society, while remaining rooted in local traditions (United Nations Working Group on Indigenous Populations 1994). Indigenous applies to European ethnic groups (e.g. the Basques) in addition to New World indigenous Nations (e.g. the Native Hawaiians).

- Globalization is a set of processes that are moving around the globe, re-shaping economic systems, political bodies, and cultural identities. Indicators of globalization are moving around the world in an uneven pattern (Giddens 2000:34). Processes of globalization are changing culture, the economy, and the State. The result is a combination of standardization, specification, and hybridization which incorporates local knowledge and cosmopolitanism.

- The global culture is dynamic. It is centered in the West, speaks English, is a partial homogenization (Hall 1997), and is influenced by the media (Appadurai 1998, Beck 2000). The global culture is constantly created and re-created. Although elements of the global culture have clear roots in the West, the global culture is not a product of Westernization. This is because the global culture is reproduced reflexively (Spybey 1996).

- Local culture refers to the culture of a particular place, a city, town, or district. Local communities are fragile: the local is bombarded with outside influences from all sides. The community must achieve a delicate balance to maintain its locality. Imagined communities conceive of elements of culture and tradition as being unique to the local context, for example traditional diet or language.

- Hybridity results when two or more cultures are incorporated to create a new cultural identity. The identities are not assimilated or altered independently—bits of identities become elements of a new identity. A third identity emerges which is not the same as the independent parts.

- Human rights encompass the right to what is minimally necessary to live (Howard 1995) and protect human agency (Ignatieff 2001). The empirical definition of human rights—what is minimally necessary to live, protects agency and agents—are socially constructed. Thus, the empirical expression of human rights is not static, but shifts as the socially defined meaning changes.

METHODOLOGY

This project explores the social phenomenon indigenousness using a case-study approach. In identifying a conceptual map for cases, Ragin (1992) identifies four understandings of cases. Cases are: found (specific-empirical), objects (general-empirical), made (specific-theoretical), or conventions (general-theoretical). Cases that are found "are empirically real and bounded, but specific" (Ragin 1992:9). If a case is an object, it is also empirically real and bounded, but does not require verification "because cases are general and conventionalize" (Ragin 1992:9–10). In the third instance, cases that are made, researchers "see cases as specific theoretical constructs which coalesce in the course of the research" (Ragin 1992:10). Finally, cases are conventions when cases are examined "as general theoretical constructs, but nevertheless view these constructions as the products of collective scholarly work and interaction, and therefore as external to any particular research effort" (Ragin 1992:10). In this project I use the Native Hawaiians as a case to make analytical contributions to the study of indigenous groups around the world. I also draw from the indigenous Mayan groups in Mexico to further illustrate the indigenous experience. This project exemplifies a process of casing as exemplified by the notion that cases

Research Design

are found and made. Indigenousness is empirically real and bounded, and it is specific. The concept of indigenousness coalesced over the course of this research project. Indigenousness is not conventionalized in sociological literatures, and thus this study does not engage in "casing" indigenous as objects or conventions.

Comparative logic is also employed to explore the breadth of indigenousness and the potential applications for this research beyond the example of the Native Hawaiians. In Chapter Six I introduce a second case, the Mayas (Zapatistas), for a comparison of the rights of indigenous Nations in the state and international doctrine. Studying a single case can weaken theoretical claims of this project. Generalizing with findings on only one case can be a risky venture. In the future I intend to study additional cases, and explore the Native Hawaiian Nation in greater depth.

DATA GATHERING EXPLAINED

The data gathering process for this project was simple in many ways. I began by looking to two reference books: *Nations Without States* (Minahan 1996) and the *World Desk Reference* (2000). Minahan's historical account of the groups gives some basic background information and a small handful of references with further information on the cases. From these books I was able to gather general information about the United States and Native Hawaiians. A third book, *Federal Indian Law* (Getches, Wilkinson, and Williams 1993) fleshed out the history of the legal relationship between the United States and Native Hawaiians, and also provided some background information on the relationship between the State of Hawai'i and Native Hawaiians. The information in these sources was not primary data, and it was very general in nature.

To gather more information, I went to the Internet, where I found countless websites on Hawai'i, Native Hawaiians, and general sites on indigenous groups. The websites vary in their content. Many of the sites on Hawai'i or Native Hawaiians are aimed at potential tourists, but others are scholarly in nature, including a link to a master's thesis, and links to the legal arguments behind the Hawaiian sovereignty movement. I created an interactive web site that lists all of the potential sources for this project I have found thus far. This web page can currently be found at http://www.unc.edu/~cedar/grpsandmvmts.html and has links to nearly 100 web sites on topics varying in specificity. Some of the pages listed are dedicated to one case and others offer general information on indigenous groups. I have subdivided them by case and topic. These websites offer links to news and historical information that can be difficult to find. Many are updated regularly to keep up with current events. Internet data must be handled more carefully, as there may be little information about the web page authors, their references, and credentials. For this reason, few of the websites are used as data sources. The websites remain useful, as they provide contextual information and show the shift in the movement as they adopt new technologies and communication strategies.

In addition to websites, the newsgroups can be a source of data. I am a member of the newsgroup called Hawai'i Nation Info, which is an efficient way of staying on top of current events. The mailing list often includes news and events postings. Being a part of this news group allows me to track the latest news on the group easily. The convenience and the community render this list a useful resource.

Finally, I have also sought materials from the literature. There is a great body of writing on Hawai'i and Native Hawaiians. I include materials by both native and non-native authors. Discussions of the Native Hawaiian experience from the voice of Native Hawaiians are not as plentiful as the other works, as there is a small community of people doing this research. Early authors were generally European, although some Native Hawaiians did write about their people (David Malo's work is one example). There are a few Native Hawaiian academics and lawyers who have written about Hawaiian sovereignty and the Hawaiian experience, which are included as references. I was also able to find articles in journals published in the region. While I was limited in some ways by the availability of materials, as East Coast libraries do not carry as many Pacific Island journals and publications, I was able to gather a large breadth of materials from a variety of sources.

CASE STUDY OF NATIVE HAWAI'I: A CASE OF WHAT?

Native Hawaiians are a unique case in the history of people indigenous to the United States. This is due to the timing of contact and acquisition of Hawai'i as a state. Because Hawai'i joined the union long after the Treaty Era ended, Native Hawaiians have a different "contract" with the federal government than the other tribes of the United States. The constitution of the State of Hawai'i dictates the terms of this relationship instead of a treaty or federal law. This relationship with the state and federal government distinguishes Native Hawaiians from other Native Americans. Below I will illustrate how the example of Native Hawaiians is an ideal case of indigenousness. This group exemplifies all ten elements of the definition of indigenous. Furthermore, their tie to the islands is uncontested since time immemorial and the legal claim of the Native Hawaiians is well documented.

Research Design

Native Hawai'i is Indigenous

Elements of the definition of indigenous are listed below in italic font, ten in all, with each one followed by a narrative of how the Native Hawaiians illustrate the concept. This discussion illustrates, in detail, how the case of Native Hawai'i exemplifies the various elements of indigenousness. This discussion demonstrates that all components of the definition of indigenous are present in the case of the Native Hawaiians.

(1) *Shared ancestry.* Hawaiians are the ancestors of the first Polynesians, probably Marquesans or Samoans, who migrated to the islands in 4th or 5th Century A.D. This is not contestable, which makes the Hawaiian case unique. The lineage of the royalty is especially uncontestable. If you wanted to trace the specific links of the monarch's family tree, this could be done.

(2) *Ancestral roots are embedded in the lands in which they live or would like to live, much more deeply than the roots of more powerful sectors of society living on the same lands or in close proximity.* The link to the land is powerful for Hawaiians, and it is not about use value or another financial element of being a landowner. The Native Hawaiians' link to the land is a tie to family, ancestors, culture, and to the self.

(3) *Common experience as colonies.* The Hawaiians are a people colonized by the United States—first as a United States territory and second as a member of the United States. The Hawaiians also have the experience of a great wave of immigration into the area: Russians, French, British, and others came to the islands mostly for economic purposes (e.g. whale hunting, shipping). Although this was not colonization, in a technical sense, it was an infringement. The numerous treaties between Hawai'i and the governments of these outsiders attest to this. Native Hawaiians share an experience of invasive immigration, as an external colony of the United States, and now as an internal colony of the United States.

(4) *Aboriginal inhabitants.* Native Hawaiians exemplify this as purely as I can imagine. Even the aborigines of Australia—due to their nomadic character—are not as "clean" an example. Again, Hawaiians are the ancestors of the first Polynesians (probably Marquesans or Samoans, more specifically) who

migrated to the islands in 4th or 5th Century A.D. This is not contestable, which makes the Hawaiian case unique. The Hawaiians were not nomads, and the islands are so small that the culture was uniform across the islands. Native Hawaiians are the only aboriginal inhabitants of the island chain.

(5) *Were living in tradition-based autonomous communities.* Native Hawaiians exemplify tradition-based elements: prior to Cook's arrival the islands were politically autonomous communities with a shared culture, norms, and values. Native Hawaiians lived in a tradition based economy, religion, culture, and political system. In 1810, Kamehameha I unified the island chain thirty-two years after Cook's arrival. The Native Hawaiians remain tradition- based as much as an existence as an internal colony has allowed them, maintaining elements of traditional religion (i.e. the worship of Lono the god of fertility), culture (i.e. traditional medicinal practices, language, *hula*, song, and many crafts), and politics (i.e. desire to return to a monarchy).

(6) *Culturally distinct.* While Native Hawaiians share many elements with other Polynesian groups, they remain distinct. There is a strong sentiment among the Native Hawaiian community about the distinction between themselves and other Polynesian communities and between themselves and the American community. Two examples illustrate the distinction between Native Hawaiians and Polynesians. A *kapa* weaving artisan, Dennis Kana'e Keawe, travels to Atiu (another Polynesian community) to share some of what he has learned about weaving. Keawe is conscious of the differences between the Hawaiian and Atiu traditions, and is careful to respect the difference and not contaminate the Atiu culture by sharing too much of the Hawaiian culture (Hartwell 1996). Another example of the Native Hawaiians' cultural distinction from other Polynesian or Pacific Islanders is the recent protests against the casting of wrestling superstar The Rock to play Kamehameha in an upcoming movie. Although The Rock's ancestry includes some Samoan roots, the Hawaiian community is outraged that a non-Hawaiian actor will be playing the part of King Kamehameha. They view The Rock as an outsider in spite of his comparatively close link to the community. The Native Hawaiians assert themselves as different from the Americans inhabiting the islands.

Although Native Hawaiians and Americans may share some uniquely Hawaiian characteristics, such as speaking Pidgin, a hybrid language including Hawaiian and English words unique to the Hawaiian Islands, this does not mean that all islanders are Native Hawaiians. The Native Hawaiians maintain a community with unique language, culture, religion, and tradition of which American Hawaiians are not a part.

(7) *Live as internal colonies.* The Hawaiians are an internal colony under the power of the United States. The State of Hawai'i is also a colonizer, as it is the body that oversees the Native Hawaiians' social services, their trust lands, and the financial issues related to the maintenance of the trust lands through the Office of Hawaiian Affairs (OHA). Much of the power that the State of Hawai'i has over Native Hawaiians was solidified with the establishment of United States sovereignty over the territory. For example, when Hawai'i became a United States territory, a law was enacted that prohibited the use of the Hawaiian language. The establishment of the Office of Hawaiian Affairs in 1978 is another example.

(8) *Incorporated elements of outside society while maintaining local traditions.* Hawaiian music incorporates the sounds of other musical genres (country western, jazz, pop, and rock) and songs may be sung in English, Pidgin, or Hawaiian. These songs often have post-colonial themes, and express Hawaiian values and norms. *Ho'oponopono* is the Hawaiian tradition of conflict resolution and forgiveness. Traditionally it was practiced amongst families and friends, and it now is also practiced in the church and in therapy. Thus, *ho'oponopono* has been incorporated into two institutions brought in by the colonial powers. These are two examples of Native Hawaiians maintaining local traditions while incorporating elements of the outside society.

(9) *Indigenous peoples are existing descendants of the peoples who inhabited the present territory of a country wholly or practically at the time when persons of a different culture or ethnic origin arrived there from other parts of the world overcame them and by conquest settlement or other means reduced them to a non-dominant or colonial situation.* Hawaiians are the ancestors of the first Polynesians (probably Marquesans or Samoans, more specifically) who migrated to the islands in 4th or 5th Century

A.D. Cook is the first known explorer to sail to the Hawaiian Islands and meet with the Hawaiian people. The people who now call themselves Native Hawaiians are descendants of the people who greeted Cook. Cook was one of a handful of explorers to sail to the islands. The explorers were followed by immigrants, who came to farm, hunt whales, spread religion, and engage in commercial shipping—to name a few things.

(10) *Indigenous peoples today live more in conformity with their particular social, economic and cultural customs and traditions than with the institutions of the country of which they now form a part, under a State structure which incorporates mainly the national, social and cultural characteristics of other segments of the populations which are predominant.* Native Hawaiians live as Americans, and for the most part are full participants in American culture while they maintain their local cultures. The Native Hawaiians continue to practice traditions such as *hula*, paddle racing, *kapa*, *kalo* farming, practice traditional medicine, observe traditional religion, and speak Hawaiian. They protest the power of the state by refusing to license their cars, or driving without State of Hawai'i driver's licenses. The Native Hawaiians are deeply invested in living in accordance with their traditional customs as much as possible.

CONCLUSION

The authenticity of Native Hawaiians, as an indigenous group, is not in doubt. Native Hawaiians have clearly established their relationship to the first inhabitants of Hawai'i. The United States' take-over of the Hawaiian monarchy and the Hawaiian Islands is clearly documented, and the circumstances surrounding this taking are largely unambiguous. The relation to ancestors of the first inhabitants of the island is documented above (see numbers 1, 5, and 9). The unlawful taking of the land is best summarized by Charles Wilkinson, as discussed in Dudley and Agard (1993). The legal case between Native Hawaiians and the United States is one of the most clean cut cases of illegal usurping of power that exists. Wilkinson, in an address to "The Native Hawaiian Rights Meeting" participants said: "no historian any longer questioned that the United States conspired against the Hawaiian government and was responsible for its overthrow" (Dudley and Agard 1993). The takeover in 1893 can be called a coup that displaced Native Sovereignty, leading to the annexation of Hawai'i in 1898. Native

Research Design

Hawaiians have the strongest claim to sovereignty of any indigenous group in the United States.

With this book I identify ten concepts and present indigenousness as a relational concept. In substantive chapters I explore the case of Native Hawai'i, which is an ideal case of indigenousness. Hawai'i embodies indigenous perfectly. There is no fighting over boundaries, as it is clear that the Hawaiians have the only claim to the territory. Prior to their arrival, the islands were uninhabited. It is an example of an indigenous group that cannot be cast in doubt. Trying to establish who was indigenous to the Gaza Strip would be nearly impossible, but here I can clearly establish that the Hawaiians were the first human occupants of the island chain. Hawai'i is an ideal type. Using the case of Hawai'i allows me to avoid tangles in issues that are tangential to the project. It holds constant the elements of indigenousness. Other groups that may not match all ten elements of the definition of indigenous may still be indigenous. Native Hawai'i is an ideal case theoretically, and in practice indigenousness may be a bit more complicated.

Chapter Three
On Indigenousness

Indigenous is not a race, an ethnicity, or a religion. Indigenous is a complex concept: as an identity, a relationship to the land and the State, and as a form of legitimation. Being indigenous is about "continuity of habitation, aboriginality, and often a 'natural' connection to the land" (Clifford 1997 [1994]: 287). This chapter begins with the presentation of a definition of indigenous and a comparison of this definition to the traditional definitions. After proposing this definition of indigenous that can be applied more widely in sociological research, I problematize indigenousness. Next, I describe indigenousness as a relational concept, and then consider the label "indigenous" as a means of legitimating communities.

DEFINE INDIGENOUSNESS

Indigenous refers to the living descendants of the pre-contact (generally contact by Europeans) aboriginal inhabitants (United Nations Working Group on Indigenous Populations 1994; Anaya 1996), who were living in tradition-based autonomous communities (Guibernau 1999). Indigenous Nations are culturally distinct (Anaya 1996, Guibernau 1999), and often live as internal colonies (Guibernau 1999), "engulfed by settler societies born of the forces of empire and conquest" (Anaya 1996:3; United Nations Working Group on Indigenous Populations 1994). In the present day, indigenous Nations have incorporated elements of the outside society, while remaining rooted in local traditions (United Nations Working Group on Indigenous Populations 1994). Indigenous people are generally only partly integrated into the State (Eriksen 1997 [1993]). Similar to this idea, it is possible to define indigenous tribes or groups as "people who deeply 'belong' in a place by dint of continuous occupancy over an extended period" (Clifford 1997 [1994]: 289). Indigenous communities should not be confused

33

with minorities because their status is not dependent upon the number of people in the community (Trask, H. 1999). The application of indigenous is broad, including European ethnic groups such as: the Basques, Irish, or Welsh; in addition to New World indigenous Nations: the Native Hawaiians, American Indians, or First Nations of Canada.

The Difference

Excluding European groups (such as the Basques or the Welsh), who are technically speaking as indigenous as groups such as the Sami or the Navajo, from definitions weakens the concept of indigenousness. This is an issue that my definition targets, by expanding the application of the definition to include all indigenous Nations—including those in the new world and those in the old world.

As I define indigenous, it can apply to groups that are viewed as colonies under the saltwater thesis, and also to the indigenous in the Old World. Under the saltwater thesis, colonialism was confined to relations overseas between a colonial power and the colonized territory. Doing so is technically relevant, as indigenous Nations do exist around the world. The concept as it is defined here does not need to be limited to the New World or former colonies under the saltwater thesis. Doing so can erode the relevance of the definition. Expanding the definition creates more opportunity for indigenous groups to gain rights and freedoms. This broader definition of the term calls for a broader application of rights due to indigenous peoples that already exist within the international governing system: for example mechanisms for the attainment of sovereignty. This change responds to Eriksen's (1997 [1993]) criticism that "the concept 'indigenous people' is thus not an accurate analytical one, but rather one drawing on broad family resemblances and contemporary political issues" (40). Instead of watering down its meaning, asserting the breadth of indigenous brings out the more technical expression of the term.

The definition of indigenous that I present here is a combination of many definitions. In writing this definition, I kept the relevant pieces and assembled them to create a new whole. The unique aspect of this definition is the assertion that it applies around the world, and is not tied to the era of European colonial expansion.

PROBLEMATIZING INDIGENOUS

Indigenous cannot be taken as unproblematic. The concept is a social and historical construct. As such, it is necessary to discuss some of the ways to problematize this term. I will address seven elements of the term, as it is defined here, that could pose a problem. Four items stem from the terminology used in the definition: pre-contact inhabitants, culturally distinct, tradition based, and inhabiting the present territory. Three other items are rooted in the empirical application of a definition of indigenousness: considering the technical definition versus the normative definition, reliance upon contested histories or imagined communities for data, and the uniformity or diversity of a community. The ways that each of these items can pose a problem in discussing indigenousness are detailed below.

1. While an essential part of defining indigenous, the requirement that a group (or individual) be living descendants of pre-contact inhabitants can be problematic. Establishing this link of familial relations can be complicated. Before contact and even in the early years of colonialism, records of familial ties existed in oral histories. If researchers do not expand their understanding of data and evidence to include information that is not written down, some indigenous peoples will be excluded. Yet, the word of mouth histories are subject to error or alteration. In the United States, censuses of American Indians were taken at various time points. These data are unreliable because of the communication gap that may have hindered counting, and it was not uncommon for people to hide their families from the government agents. Racism on the part of officials also limits the information available in some circumstances. The potential for errors renders it difficult to offer reliable evidence of familial ties to pre-contact inhabitants with oral histories or census data. Supporting or denying a group or individual the status of "indigenous" is a challenge in the best circumstance.

2. Similarly, the element of a distinct culture is a part of what it means to be indigenous and must be included in the definition. But establishing that a group is culturally distinct becomes more difficult with globalization. Standardization is spreading, and in many ways this includes cultural standardization. But localities remain distinct, sometimes in only subtle ways. Many indigenous groups continue to maintain a distinct community: perhaps by protecting stories or an artisan's technique. They have local knowledge that allows them to survive cyclones ("Solomon survivors tell their story" 2003) in the Solomon Islands and predict the weather in Australia ("Experts look to Australia's Aborigines for weather help" 2003). Even with contact from outsiders, the

indigenous communities are distinct. This might be less evident when the people wear Levi's jeans as opposed to rawhide pants or dresses woven of cedar bark. It may require more digging to find data that illustrate the difference, but this does not mean that there is no distinction.

3. The requirement that an indigenous group be tradition based is another element of the definition that is problematic. When talking about this portion of the definition, it is important to allow space for societies to change. Culture and identity are not static. They change over time, as a result of influences from within as well as outside of the communities. While this change might shift the expression of culture, it does not necessarily eliminate the existence of the group. Establishing what it means to be tradition based in a globalizing society is an empirical problem. This question was asked recently in the Pacific Northwest, where the Makah tribe petitioned for and won the right to carry on a whale hunt. This was within their treaty rights, as it was deemed a usual and accustomed practice. Observers criticized the tribe for their use of firearms and motorboats instead of spears and canoes. Yet, the Makah argued that the use of modern conveniences did not render the hunt non-traditional (i.e. in their usual and accustomed practices). The ceremonial elements of the whale hunt did follow tradition. Other questions of authenticity will arise as indigenous groups are modernizing. This can sometimes result in a "non-authentic" tax, the idea that the group is not authentic if they make use of modern technology. Researchers must carefully consider what it means to be "tradition based" with whatever data they can gather. The fluid nature of collective identity must be considered to ensure that indigenous Nations are tradition based, while not excluding groups that modernize at varying rates.

4. The final text from the definition that will be discussed here is the requirement that an indigenous group be existing descendants of peoples who inhabited the present territory at the time when the outsiders arrived. This might be repaired by a careful syntactical shift. It is important that the group be the residents of a given territory upon the arrival of another group. However, the indigenous group may not inhabit the same territory in present times. In many cases, settlers or the governments forced indigenous peoples off the land. As such, at this point in time they may not inhabit

the territory that their indigenous roots link them to. The problem is the notion of being descendants of peoples who inhabit the "present territory" if this is applied in a literal manner. Substituting the term "contested" for "present" might improve the precision of the definition.

5. In talking about indigenousness, there is discord between the meaning of the term in theory and in the normative behavior. To explain this more clearly I will present an example. It is possible for an American Indian tribe to exist, but to have no political rights as a tribe because the norms established within the federal acknowledgement process exclude the tribe from achieving recognition. The Golden Hill Indians of Connecticut are one example. Many indigenous communities find themselves outside the boundaries of the normative system, either state or international. This leaves them in a vulnerable circumstance, often experiencing unequal distribution due to their ascribed identity as indigenous, without the protections that are awarded to groups that fall within the normative boundaries. There are protections for indigenous peoples in many international legal documents and often in State legal documents, but the groups and individual members find themselves in a void. They normatively fall outside of a system designed to protect them and their cultural identity. In defining indigenous, I choose to base the definition upon empirical evidence, but it is possible to argue that the definition should instead match the system of norms.

6. The reliance upon contested histories and imagined communities for data renders the assessment of groups as indigenous or not problematic. The real world is messy and it is not simple to determine which community is indigenous to a given territory. Cultural boundaries are blurry. An example that is in the news almost daily is the dispute between the Israelis and the Palestinians. Both claim historical ties to territory, and for each community the sites hold religious significance. It is not possible to establish one side as having a greater right to indigenousness. There is no way to state which version is the more truthful or real version of history, because it is in the past and we only have evidence to support hypotheses. In many cases there is support for both sides. The firm establishment of a group as

being indigenous can be impossible in some circumstances, due to a lack of reliability in the data that are required to make an assessment.

This makes it difficult to apply any technical norms or standards, because the simple act of determining who or what they apply to may be more difficult than what the standards recognize (i.e. the federal acknowledgment process in the United States). Everything is shared, boundaries are unclear, and communications and technology are standardizing and allowing for a sort of standardizing among the cultures. Establishing indigenous requires that we rely upon imagined communities and imagined histories. They all have truth and realism, and can cause there to be real consequences. Thus, the firm establishment of a group as being indigenous empirically is perhaps impossible, with the exception of a few ideal types.

7. Although it might be implied that indigenous groups are uniform, they are not. Within a single community, the people might be diverse due to intermarriage, variance in income or class, gender inequalities, or disputes between traditional and cosmopolitan members. Many tribes in the Northwest have had vitriolic disputes over casino building projects. Often one side is promoting gaming for its potential as an economic resource and another side is fearful of the risk of tribal members becoming addicted to gambling. In explorer's journals I have seen descriptions of Northwest Indian people shortly after contact. They describe two types: the "hang around the forts" and the "traditional" Indians. While indigenous peoples are one type of group, there is great diversity within the population of indigenous peoples, or within tribes, bands, or Nations. Similarly, there are differences among feminists, civil rights groups, or political parties. An indigenous group is not completely uniform or homogeneous. Yet, like political parties, the feminist movement, or civil rights groups, indigenous peoples remain a unified front on certain issues. Their diversity does not render them unable to act as a collective, and it does not erode their collective identity.

THE RELATIONAL CONCEPT

Indigenous is in part reliant upon the relation to another power or body in order to be established. Being colonized is about being taken advantage of, about losing freedoms: it is an invasion. As a result of the colonial

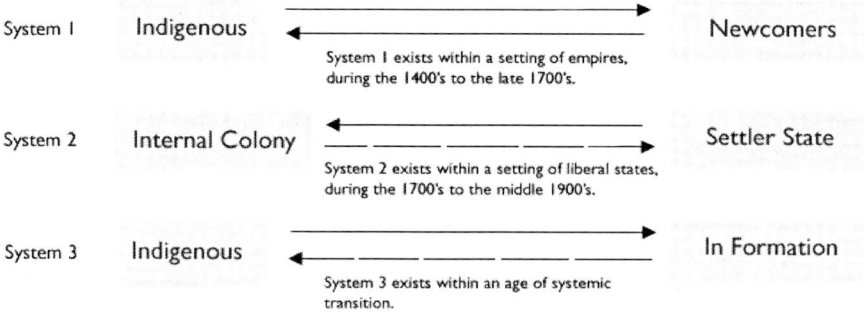

Figure 3.1 The Relational Concept: Three Systems

experience, lands were stolen, cultures were assimilated, the language was nearly lost, the right to self-govern was taken, and people now live in the shadow of what they once were. There are three key ways that indigenous is a relational concept: Indigenous to Newcomers, Internal Colonies to the Settler State, and Indigenous to "In Formation" (see Figure 3.1). These relationships can be described as three different systems. In the first system, indigenous and newcomers both have reciprocating directional arrows to indicate some level of reciprocity between the two. In the second system, internal colonies and the settler State have a less egalitarian relationship, which is illustrated by a dotted arrow running from internal colonies to the settler state and a solid arrow running in the opposite direction. In the final system, the indigenous and "in formation" are again opposing each other in an unequal relationship, but this time there is a solid arrow running from indigenous to "in formation" and a dotted arrow running in the reverse direction. All of the systems exist within a setting of the capitalist world economy, which is now in an age of transition. Each system exists in an era dominated by one type of political body: for the first system this is the empire, for the second system it is the liberal State, and for the third system it is the liberal empire. When system one becomes politicized it shifts to a relationship as described in system two. When system two becomes globalized it shifts to a relationship as described in system three.

The colonial period began with the shifting of populations around the world following the explorations of the 1400s. There was not a concept of indigenous prior to European expansion. My dictionary cites the birth of the term as 1646, which is well after initial European explorations. Prior to this experience, indigenous groups were independent Nations, tribes, or bands, and did not share a collective identity such as Pan-Indian or indigenous. In the early days of interaction between Europeans and Indians, neither side identified any difference within the population of the outsiders (Wilmer 1997 [1993]). That is, Indians did not recognize the different nationalities of the explorers, and the explorers did not recognize different tribal identities among the Indians. Since then, pan-European and pan-Indian subconscious has become a source of identity in the global context (Wilmer 1997 [1993]). This is a relational concept: between the original peoples of the land since recorded history, to the later arrivals to the land—now the colonial powers (Maaka and Fleras 2000).

The majority of indigenous peoples live as internal colonies. They are citizens of the State, but this State is the one created by the settler societies that formed as a result of colonialism. It is in many ways a foreign State that grew up around them. Hawai'i came under United States jurisdiction via a hostile taking of the land and sovereignty. The queen surrendered her sovereignty, in lieu of seeing her people die. The people, who did not surrender sovereignty, have been subjected to the United States rule for nearly one hundred years. The colonial era continues, with internal colonies. Indigenous Nations of the Americas were first external colonies to the British, Spanish, and French powers. The indigenous peoples-settler state relations "confirms indigenous policy as a 'contested domain' involving the struggle of opposing interests for definition and control" (Maaka and Fleras 2000:96). For indigenous peoples their context, internal colonies living within settler states, illustrates the relational aspect of indigenousness.

In the world-system there are three structural positions: core, periphery, and semi-periphery. Wallerstein (2000) describes each of these three positions. Countries in the core of the economic structure are generally more sophisticated industrially, diverse in agricultural production, and specialize in skilled labor, using wage-labor to control labor. Countries in the periphery of the economic structure tend to specialize in agriculture (especially grains, cotton, sugar, or wood) and bullion production, which favor harsh labor controls such as slavery and cash crop labor. Countries in the semi-periphery of the economic structure tend to specialize in high-cost industrial products, credit, and specie transactions using share cropping and minimizing of exports to control labor. Entities other than countries can also fall under the three economic positions in the world-system, such as international regions or sub-state regions.

The capitalist world economy has been in existence since 1450, and is shifting to a period of terminal crisis (Wallerstein 1999). The world-system is now in a structural crisis, and is moving into a period of transition (Wallerstein 2002). The capitalist economy was able to sustain itself for 500 years by installing mechanisms that restore equilibrium. But with each restoration the equilibrium shifted. Three trends, which cannot be resolved, will push the system into crisis. These trends are the real wage level as a percentage of the costs of production (in the world-system as a whole); the cost of material inputs; and taxation levels (Wallerstein 1999). Pressures on profit levels, the cost of material inputs (rising due to the cost of clean-up and/or organic renewal), and taxation rates threaten the accumulation of capital. In this setting of economic pressure, the capitalist world-system is also finding itself threatened by anti-statism (Wallerstein 1999). In the atmosphere of anti-statism, security concerns are heightened and people are relying less heavily upon the State to protect them, and States are experiencing delegitimation. These two consequences of anti-statism are a threat to capitalists in two ways: a spiral of greater violence and lesser ability of the State to regulate violence is the result; and the State is less able to control the "dangerous classes" which threaten the capitalists (Wallerstein 1999). The crisis will either result in a more democratic and egalitarian world-system, or a different system that perpetuates the strength of those in power.

This is an interesting time to be in the core, periphery, or semi-periphery of the world-system. Using the example of Native Hawaiians, both the United States and the State of Hawai'i are in the core position, and the Native Hawaiians are in the periphery. Many other indigenous Nations find themselves in the periphery of the world-system, as they most likely embraced capitalism later and experience oppression that inhibits their achievements. While this is a disadvantage in the capitalist world economy as it exists today, indigenous Nations may emerge in a different position following the age of transition. Embracing pluralism, adopting hybrid identities, an increasingly international voice, along with a distinct worldview might enable indigenous Nations to navigate the conflict with success. Exactly what indigenous Nations will find themselves in relation to at the end of the crisis is still in formation.

These are a few ways that indigenous can be described as relational. Other ways that might be examined further in the future include: government-to-government, a cultural distinction (especially the differing worldview), immigrants and non-immigrants, and it is a political otherness—outside of the system of citizenship. Within the concept of indigenous there are relational concepts that can be analyzed as well, such as the one between the local identity and the pan-Indian or pan-indigenous identity. This begins to expose the complexity of this as a topic of study.

CAN INDIGENOUS LEGITIMATE?

Indigenous groups and others are seeking legitimacy and recognition. The acknowledgement of indigenous status can bring economic, social, and political benefits. For this reason, the label indigenous can be an asset. The label indigenous does give credence to recognized Nations, tribes or bands. Yet, it does not legitimate a group that lacks other political backing (e.g. federal or international recognition), regardless of the strength of the claims. Indigenousness might be a frame that groups or individuals wish to employ in order to gain political and economic advantage. Below I describe how indigenous does not legitimate the claims of: indigenous groups with historical claims but no political support or non-indigenous peoples seeking rights that indigenous peoples enjoy. This is followed by a description of how the label indigenous does legitimate recognized indigenous groups with legal, social, and political authority.

The label or term indigenous does not legitimate groups that have historical claims to the label but lack the political support—from other local tribes, from state governments, or from federal governments. Claims for self-determination on the international stage are subject to the social construct of the meaning of Nation and indigenous. Indigenous Nations' pleas for self-determination are more likely to be acknowledged if the group is not located within the bounds of an established State (Hechter and Borland 2001). Groups may have relevant claims, but if their form or shape is not in accordance with the norms, the likelihood of achieving success decreases. Thus, some indigenous groups fall between the cracks within the State and within the international community of States.

The term does not legitimate non-indigenous peoples, either. Instead, when non-indigenous groups appropriate the term—as a political strategy, a form of flattery or alliance, or for some other reason—it erodes the precision and authority of the term. The improper use of this term takes something away from indigenous peoples. This is a part of why indigenous peoples challenge new groups attempting to gain legitimacy,[1] or individuals trying to enter the group as a member. There is very strict gate keeping in effect among indigenous peoples. It is an important border that they guard. State and international systems also create rigorous standards to protect themselves and minimize their responsibilities. For non-indigenous peoples, co-opting the label indigenous cannot legitimate.

Indigenous does legitimate the claims of identity of groups who wear the label with legal, social, and political authority. This is why other groups and individuals seek to employ the label indigenous. The term indigenous can legitimate groups that are recognized as such by the settler state, or the international political system. But it is not the term "indigenous" that legitimates the group, but the recognition of the term by a political organization with power that legitimates it. For groups that are recognized as an indigenous group, their local identity is primary, and their status as indigenous is secondary.

A more critical response to this question suggests that indigenousness is not only about being indigenous. Instead, it is also "a process of identification in the contemporary global arena that is a powerful expression of the transformation of the global system" (Friedman 1999:408). In this situation a group asserts itself as indigenous for politically strategic reasons, instead of as a cultural identity. In other cases, individuals assert their identity as religion by engaging in indigenous religious rituals. Identity that is not solely ethnic or cultural in nature is challenged, for being "territorial as well, and they are critical aspects of the new turf wars in the cities and the ethnic wars in both Europe, and in Africa" (Friedman 1999: 408–409). This critique does not allow for the inclusion of territory as an element of identity, implicitly asserting that identity stops at the person. In limiting the boundaries of identity, it forces a limit in the identity of indigenous groups.

CONCLUSION

Globalization and the questioning of traditional values and modernization have made indigenous peoples visible (Guibernau 1999). Their experience as internal colonies is gaining attention in international non-government organizations and in international governing organizations. Policies are being enacted to protect indigenous peoples and their cultures. Organizations such as UNESCO are working to revitalize and maintain cultures. The United Nations is working to expand indigenous political rights, especially in regards to political sovereignty. Yet, indigenous peoples will only be truly decolonized when it is recognized that indigenous identity is a dynamic process (Barcham 2000). Instead of being tied to nostalgic images of indigenous, such as the Hollywood Indian, the culture and people will be free to modernize without challenges to authenticity.

Chapter Four
The Hawaiians

The case of Native Hawai'i stands out because it is one of the indigenous groups in the United States that has strong nationalist sentiment with goals that include seeking statehood. The people who today call themselves Native Hawaiians migrated to the island chain from Samoa sometime between the fifth and ninth centuries and larger migrations joined them between the twelfth and fifteenth centuries (Minahan 1996). Native Hawaiians are in a "relationship between ourselves and those who want control of us *and* our resources is not a *formerly* colonial relationship but an *ongoing* colonial relationship" (Trask, H.[1] 1999: 103). After cultural renewal movements in the 1950s and 1960s, the 1970s brought nationalist sentiment to the Native Hawaiians (Minahan 1996). Native Hawaiians have remained at the bottom of the economic, social, and political ladders since their Queen lost power (Getches et al 1993; Minahan 1996).

Support is growing for a Hawaiian Nation and for the sovereignty movement. Hawaiians seek sovereignty for three reasons: the United States violated international law when it made Hawai'i a state, the United States has not protected the Hawaiian people as a benevolent democratic government ought to, and Hawaiians have a right to remain in their homeland (Dudley and Agard 1993). Hawaiians seek land or compensation, calling upon Hawaiian tradition, in which "land is sacred, the state's unbridled growth, environmental destruction, and growing pollution [is] considered blasphemy" (Minahan 1996: 228). This chapter will detail some of the highlights of the Hawaiian political history since contact. I divide the chapter into sections that describe the Hawaiian experience: Independent Hawai'i, Land, and The Hawaiian Renaissance to Present Day.

INDEPENDENT HAWAI'I

The Polynesians were the world's most venturesome explorers, spreading their populace across a triangle that included the area between Hawai'i, Easter Island, and New Zealand (Kuykendall and Day 1948). A first migration to Hawai'i occurred in 400 A.D., and a second migration occurred between the early eleventh century and the late fourteenth centuries (Kuykendall and Day 1948). The newcomers became the dominant members of society, as their chiefs took over leadership roles and their priests became spiritual leaders (Kuykendall and Day 1948). Following this second immigration, the Hawaiian Islands were again isolated, and "the history of these centuries is full of the adventures of the *ali'i*, male and female, and the details of the battles that were fought in their quest for supremacy" (Kuykendall and Day 1948:7). The island group consisted of four kingdoms: Hawai'i, Maui, Oahu, and Kauai (Kuykendall and Day 1948). Each island was its own political and economic unit and averaged a population of 30,000 (Sahlins 1958). The chiefs were known to be despotic (Malo 1951; Sahlins 1958). The smaller islands were either independent or prizes of war. The chiefs occasionally attempted to unite the islands, but only Kamehameha achieved this (Kuykendall and Day 1948). War was frequent as rival chiefs battled for ruling powers, and the commoners served as warriors when the chief went to war (Kuykendall and Day 1948).

The stratification system in Hawai'i consisted of three classes (Sahlins 1958), the high chiefs (*ali'i*), their families, and the separate political leaders on each island were one class. Local stewards, who were often relatives of the paramount chief (island chiefs), made up the second class. The third class consisted of the commoners. This was the largest class. There was also a small "outcaste" group, which consisted of those who broke laws (*tabus*) or conquered peoples. High chiefs and their family most likely did not contribute to the subsistence production (Sahlins 1958). The commoners were the major source of labor because "anyone of higher status could call upon those under him to contribute labor for communal enterprises" (Sahlins 1958:16). There was a division of labor along gender lines, with the men providing food for the household and the women caring for children, weaving mats, and making clothing (Kuykendall and Day 1948). The Hawaiian way of life was parallel to feudalism in medieval Europe, with the exception of religion (Kuykendall and Day 1948). There was no middle class, only a ruling elite and the commoners. The commoners were prosperous under a complex redistributive hierarchy (Sahlins 1958). Yet, luxury goods were only distributed to the members of the higher classes and quality of housing varied with class status (Sahlins 1958).

The Hawaiians

The Hawaiian Islands have five vegetation zones (Sahlins 1958) that allows for a diversity of plant resources. People farmed *taro*, sweet potato, banana, yam, breadfruit, sugar cane, coconut, pandanus, candlenut, arrowroot, and ti (Kuykendall and Day 1948; Sahlins 1958). People also raised fish in *taro* terraces. The seashore provided a food source (Kuykendall and Day 1948). There were seasonal shortages of some particular food items, but no major decline in the amount of food (Sahlins 1958). With the exception of rare instances of localized famine, subsistence level was maintained (Sahlins 1958).

The Hawaiian language is a local variant of the Polynesian language (Kuykendall and Day 1948). The language was spoken only, and thus songs and chants charted genealogies, stories, and traditions (Kuykendall and Day 1948). Travel amongst the islands was popular, and "welcoming a visitor was ingrained in the Hawaiian nature" (Kuykendall and Day 1948). Hawaiians enjoyed surfing, sledding, swimming, *hula*, bowling (a Hawaiian version), foot-racing, boxing and wrestling (Kuykendall and Day 1948).

Extended families were patrilocal (Sahlins 1958). Chiefs had larger families. Hawaiians respect each other and shared resources (Maunupau 1994:46). The communal nature of the Hawaiian people is evident in the words that they use to describe leprosy. In Hawaiian, it is called *ma'i ho'oka'awale*, the separating sickness. Leprosy was called the separating sickness because the disfigurement of this disease was the emotional pain of being separated from loved ones and not being able to care for the ill (Gomes 1994). Native Hawaiian society has long valued strong family relationships, known as the *'ohana* spirit (Maunupau 1994).

When James Cook first arrived at the islands in 1778, Hawai'i was not unified, but was a group of islands with independent leadership on each island (Getches et al 1993; Minahan 1996). The moral order was based upon a system of sacred law known as *kapu* (Trask, H. 1999). The economy was based upon balanced use of the resources of the land and sea. The family was the economic base and also established the network of chiefs, or *ali'i* (Trask, H. 1999). Hawai'i had a land tenure system similar to feudal Europe, granting the commoners a few more rights in the form of the freedom to move if a landlord was unfair, and the idea that land is held for the common good (Getches et al 1993: 945). Under this system, royalty owned land in slices that started at the mountain peaks and extended outwards to the ocean (Trask, H. 1999). Laborers worked the land, but were not required to maintain a permanent residence with any landholder (Trask, H. 1999). This relationship gave the laborers the power to demand fair treatment (Trask, H. 1999). Within this system, reciprocity maintained the relationships between landowner and laborer, royalty and commoner.

Cook's arrival brought a changing tide of "depopulation; foreign exploitation; cultural conflict; adoption of harmful foreign ways; and neglect, insensitivity, and malice from the ruling establishment" (Blaisdell and Mokuau 1994:50). "Leaders and the chiefs were awed and very impressed with the technology, the materials, the boats, the clothing, the ships, and the guns and cannons, the foreigners brought" (Maunupau 1994). Their quick adoption of the new technologies contributed to the loss of Native Hawaiian culture (Maunupau 1994).

Kamehameha united the islands in 1810, when King Kaumaulii of Kauai ceded his island. Hawaiians regard Kamehameha as a hero for uniting the islands (Kuykendall and Day 1948). Upon establishing his rule of the islands, Kamehameha distributed the lands and resources and continued in the Hawaiian tradition of leadership (Kuykendall and Day 1948). The years of war leading up to the uniting of the islands left the islands in a ruined condition, with a widespread famine weakening the people (Kuykendall and Day 1948). Kamehameha worked quickly to restore the islands and the islanders. The health and wealth of the islands was restored (Kuykendall and Day 1948). Kamehameha dealt fairly with foreign traders. Kamehameha maintained the local religion, including the infrastructure in buildings and law (Kuykendall and Day 1948). Kamehameha died in 1819 and Liholiho became King (Kuykendall and Day 1948).

Americans arrived to harvest sandalwood in the 1820's (Trask, H. 1999). American Protestant missionaries began arriving in 1820 and sent the *kahuna*, the Hawaiian intelligentsia and spiritual leaders, underground (Pitzer 1998 [1984]). In 1825 the first sugar and coffee plantations were started in Hawai'i. Japanese, Portuguese, Filipino and Chinese workers came to the islands as plantation workers on lands owned by American missionaries (Minahan 1996). In 1834 the Great *Mahele* took place under the leadership of Kamehameha III (more information on this in the "land" section). Whaling was a big portion of the economy briefly in the 1840's (Trask, H. 1999). The sugar plantations grew during the Civil War, which prohibited exports of sugar from the American south to the American north.

The Kingdom of Hawai'i was formally recognized by the United States in 1842. In 1851 King Kamehameha III signed a secret agreement that placed the islands under the protection of the United States. Hawai'i had signed numerous treaties, which are evidence of its independence and agency as a State. Treaties with United States were signed in 1826, 1849, 1875, and 1884. Hawai'i also had treaties with Great Britain, France, Denmark, Hamburg, Sweden and Norway, Tahiti, Belgium, Netherlands, Italy, Spain, Swiss Confederation, Russia, Japan, Portugal, Hong Kong, and

Samoa. In 1875 the Hawaiians signed a reciprocity treaty with the United States, allowing sugar and other products to enter the United States without customs duties (the U.S. Senate ratified this treaty in 1876).

Hawaiian leadership was less stable towards the end of the 1800's. Many of the monarchs became ill and died after serving short terms. Some of them become ill while traveling and others are sickened on the islands. In 1887 the erosion of Hawaiian power began: "together with the cession of Pearl River Lagoon, the Bayonet Constitution effectively challenged the sovereignty of the Kingdom" (Trask, H. 1999: 11). The Bayonet Constitution was singed by King Kalakaua, at gunpoint, in 1887. Hawaiians revolted, seeking amendments to the Bayonet Constitution (Trask, H. 1999). Robert Wilcox, a half-Hawaiian man, led Hawaiian troops in an insurrection to restore the power of the king (Dudley and Agard 1993). American troops restored order. Wilcox was tried for treason but was acquitted by a jury of Hawaiians (Dudley and Agard 1993).

In 1890 the McKinley Act, legislation privileging Hawaiian sugar imports, was put into law (Dudley and Agard 1993). The timing of this act coincides with Manifest Destiny on the continent. Hawaiian leadership sought to protect sovereignty from the outsiders, signing treaties with France, Great Britain, and the United States to ensure Hawaiian independence (Trask, H. 1999). Dudley and Agard (1993) contend that this act was designed to "cause enough major problems in Hawai'i that the Annexationists would have "just cause" to overthrow the Queen. Hawai'i could then be annexed" (55). An economic depression followed, and the annexationists gained strength. American planters pushed for annexation, while the Hawaiians protested it. The missionaries might have also played a role in the expansionism, following the guidance of their supporters on the mainland: politicians (former governors and congress members) and merchandisers and shippers (Dudley and Agard 1993). The McKinley Act was repealed in 1894.

Queen Lili'uokalani, who came into power in 1891, was under great pressure to give her people a new constitution (Trask, H. 1999). Her efforts to achieve this were thwarted, and Hawai'i was annexed on February 1, 1893 (Trask, H. 1999). President Cleveland withdrew this annexation on March 4, 1893, yet Queen Lili'uokalani was never restored to power (Trask, H. 1999). Hawai'i came under United States jurisdiction via this hostile taking of the land and sovereignty. The queen surrendered her sovereignty, in lieu of seeing her people die. The people, who did not surrender sovereignty, have been subjected to the United States rule for nearly one hundred years.

Instead, in 1894 the Republic of Hawai'i was formed, with Sanford B. Dole as president. Dole was inaugurated under a sign reading "Westward the course of empire" (Dudley and Agard 1993). As the republic was establishing itself, resistance continued. In 1895, Wilcox led another attempted take-over of the government to return it to Hawaiians (Dudley and Agard 1993). This attempt also failed, and the Queen abdicated her throne to protect Wilcox and his royalists from death sentences (Dudley and Agard 1993). In 1897 a document called the "Monster Petition," a petition protesting annexations signed by 29,000 Native Hawaiians, was sent to the United States congress (Dudley and Agard 1993). The petition seemingly fell upon deaf ears. United States President McKinley signed the Treaty of Annexation (to annex Hawai'i) in 1897, but it was never ratified by congress (Dudley and Agard 1993). Hawai'i's sovereignty was formally transferred to the United States in 1898 when it was annexed by law in a legislative bill called the Newland Resolution (Dudley and Agard 1993). The Territory of Hawai'i's first legislature convened in 1901.

Plantation owners had political dominance and an ally in the President. Following annexation, Hawaiians created an oppositional democratic party, creating "a political unit within the construct of the American two-party system" (Trask, H. 1999: 65). Under the idea that political power would be limited for Hawaiians as long as it remained a territory, the democratic party of Hawai'i pushed for statehood. If Hawai'i were a state, the governor would wield the power, instead of the president. Hawaiians were active in the push for statehood. Attaining United States citizenship would hopefully grant Native Hawaiians rights and greater political control (Trask, H. 1999).

December of 1941 marked the Japanese attack on Pearl Harbor. In 1944 the United States Democratic National Convention endorsed statehood for Hawai'i, and in 1948 President Harry S. Truman endorsed statehood for Hawai'i. With the hopes of obtaining statehood, in April 1950 the Hawai'i Constitution Convention convened. Hawai'i joined the union in 1959 (Trask, H. 1999). After a long fight on both sides, Hawaiians became a conquered people in their homeland. The final decision was made by the United States Congress and President, and a vote on the islands to either become a member of the United States or remain a U.S. territory. At this time, Native Hawaiians "were encouraged to "become American," and many did" (Dudley and Agard 1993: 73). The Hawaiian language was prohibited under the new territorial government. Hawaiians were Americanized, as children began to attend American schools and the American media began to spread.

Hawai'i had been on the United Nations' list of non-self-governing territories, with all of the privileges accorded to non-self-governing peoples by the United Nations. With statehood, the United States quietly asked

The Hawaiians 51

for Hawai'i to be removed from the list (Dudley and Agard 1993). Unlike mainland tribes, the Native Hawaiians did not have a treaty relationship with the federal government. Provisions did exist for the rights of Native Hawaiians, but they limit the rights of Native Hawaiians to negotiate on their own behalf—instead only the federal government can act (Getches et al 1993). Native Hawaiians have remained at the bottom of the economic, social, and political ladders since their Queen lost power (Getches et al 1993; Minahan 1996).

LAND

I locate my discussion of land in the middle of the chapter because it lies at the heart of the Hawaiians' goals for sovereignty, and it is at the core of the Hawaiian experience. For Native Hawaiians, the land is an ancestor. In this belief system, "nature was not objectified but personified, resulting in an extraordinary respect for the life of the sea, the heavens, and the earth" (Trask, H. 1999: 5). For the capitalist state, land is a rare and valuable commodity on this island.

Prior to colonization, Hawaiians lived under a land tenure system. Commoners maintained plots stretching from the seashore to the mountains (Sahlins 1958). The high chiefs and the local stewards supervised the access to land and water (Sahlins 1958). "Before Kamehameha, the areas were intact as ahupua'a [land divisions that usually extended from the mountains to the sea], and people loved, respected, and took care of their own areas" (Uprichard 1998 [1988]: 315). In this system, famine was rare and extended family units shared resources. The chief oversaw a hierarchical redistributive system. Commoners did the majority of the labor on the lands.

Colonial influences forced the end to this landholder system in 1843 (Trask, H. 1999). Under King Kamehameha III, the Great *Mahele* transformed the land tenure system from traditional to the Western-style of private property ownership. The Great *Mahele* reflected an ideological colonialism (Dudley and Agard 1993). At the time of the Great *Mahele* Kamehameha III set aside lands: crown lands and government lands. Some lands were allocated to the royals, which would be maintained for the common good in the tradition of the Hawaiian relationship to the land. Other lands were kept in trust to be allocated to qualified Native Hawaiian families. This left a lot of extra land available to merchants, farmers, and missionaries. Thus, with the Great *Mahele*, land was freed up for the taking. "By 1888, three-quarters of all arable land was controlled by *haole*" (Trask, H. 1999: 7).[2] The Great *Mahele* was not unlike the process of putting American Indians on reservations and paying for the remainder of the lands that the government confiscated.

Upon annexation, lands were ceded to the United States by the Republic of Hawai'i, to be held in trust for the Hawaiian people (Dudley and Agard 1993). Native Hawaiians were not asked for permission to cede the lands, and they did not surrender their claim to the land. The total ceded land area consisted of roughly half of the eight major islands.

The state has done poorly in its management of the ceded lands. The Hawaiian Homes Commission Act of 1920 set aside 200,000 acres for Native Hawaiians (Dudley and Agard 1993, Hartwell 1996, Trask, H. 1999). The lands set aside were the least desirable on the island—far from water and too rocky to farm easily (Hartwell 1996). Blood quantum was established in 1921 by the U.S. Congress (Heckathorn 1998 [1988]). When lands were set aside for the Hawaiian Homelands, Congress established that only individuals with 50% blood quantum were entitled to apply for land (Hartwell 1996; Heckathorn 1998 [1988]). When Hawai'i became a state in 1959, the text of the Act admitting Hawai'i to the union required the state to hold the trust lands and the income from the lands (Getches, Wilkinson and Williams 1993). The income from leased properties was to be used for education, to improve the conditions of the Native Hawaiians, to develop farm and home ownership, and to provide lands for public use (Getches, Wilkinson and Williams 1993).

Government agencies lease twenty-nine thousand acres, and ninety-three thousand five hundred acres are leased to non-beneficiaries for commercial, industrial, or other uses (Hartwell 1996). Almost twenty percent of the acreage is used for federal use, such as for military bases and parks (Dudley and Agard 1993). The funds from these leases do not even cover the expenses of the Department of Hawaiian Homelands (Trask, H. 1994 [1992]; Hartwell 1996). The Office of Hawaiian Affairs, which was created during the state's constitutional convention to oversee the trust, continues to mismanage the funds and the land. This constitutes an abuse of Hawaiian Homelands trust lands.

Over twenty-nine thousand applications were on file for pastoral and residential lots in 1998 (Trask, H. 1999). Yet as Hartwell (1996) describes, over one hundred thirty thousand acres of trust lands were being used illegally (Trask, H. 1999). Only forty thousand four hundred of the total acres have been distributed to eligible Native Hawaiians (Hartwell 1996). Many Native Hawaiians still do not have lands that are due to them under the Hawaiian Homelands law. The wait for property to become available is long. Because Native Hawaiians are regarded as wards of the state, they cannot challenge the illegal use of lands in state or federal courts (Trask,

H. 1999). Adequate trust lands were not allocated early in statehood, and today the majority of Native Hawaiians are on a waiting list for homelands instead of enjoying the benefits. Today eighty-two landowners own ninety-five percent of the land on Hawai'i, two of which are the federal and state governments, which own over fifty percent of the land (Trask, M. 1994). The remaining 80 private landowners own forty-seven percent of the land (Trask, M. 1994). This leaves very little of a precious resource.

For the Native Hawaiians

According to the Hawaiian worldview, Native Hawaiians "trace their origins to Kumulipo (dark source), with the mating of Wākea, the sky father, to Papa, the earth mother, from which everything in the cosmos was born and continues to be derived" (Blaisdell and Mokuau 1994). The Hawaiian creation story shows that Hawaiians are related to the land, as they would be to other humans. Genealogical ties link the islands and the people. Evidence of this exists in the way that Hawaiians speak about the land in their native language. When qualifying nouns in Hawaiian, the "a" possessive indicates acquired status and the use of the "o" possessive designates inherent status (Trask, H. 1999). Inherent status is used to refer to one's family, one's body, and the land: "in our way of speaking, land is inherent to the people; it is like our bodies and our parents" (Trask, H. 1999: 116). In this manner, nature and land are personified (Trask, H. 1999). Hawaiians are children of the land (Trask, H. 1994 [1992]), and this familial tie to the land is at the core of the relationship between Native Hawaiians and the Hawaiian Islands.

The traditional law of the land was to love and care for the land (Blaisdell and Mokuau 1994). Native Hawaiians were stewards (Aluli and McGregor 1994; Blaisdell and Mokuau 1994), not owners of the land, and it was their responsibility to care for the lands for future generations (Blaisdell and Mokuau 1994). The subsistence economy required mutual caring (Blaisdell and Mokuau 1994). The decline of Native Hawaiians is traced to the dispossession of lands (Trask, H. 1994 [1992]; Uprichard 1998; Aoudé 1999). Hawaiians must regain control of their lands to end this downward trend. To re-establish the Hawaiian way of life they must regain the lands, "the land is the core of Hawaiian identity today" (Hasager and Friedman 1994:10). For Hawaiians the land is more than a commodity or an entitlement. Land is culturally invaluable. The defense of land is urgent.

For the United States

The Hawaiian Islands provide land that is important to the United States due to the strategic advantage of a land base in the Pacific Ocean. This advantage remains important as relations with North Korea, most recently, are tenuous. As the war on terrorism has the potential to expand in Asia, the bases on Hawai'i will be essential. The United States stands to lose a great military foothold if all of Hawai'i were to secede from the United States, or if the Native Hawaiians asserted their rights to the trust lands that are presently occupied by the United States military.

The tourism industry exacerbates the economic importance of the land, especially waterside and other scenic properties. Burial grounds have been displaced by resort properties. Tourism has also contributed to the scarcity of water. Water rights have been a problem for Native Hawaiians in the revival of *kalo* farming. Because of the limited access to water resources, it has been difficult to revive this traditional way of life (which remains uniquely traditional because it is an entirely manual process, and it produces a traditional element of the diet—*poi*). Finally, the tourism industry creates a need to maintain an image that resonates with stereotypes. The island has to embody a paradise, and thus any discord can have a greater cost to the government and the state.

Economic Impact

Indigenous groups have been exposed to external societies prior to globalization. While the globalization processes might be new, and may create new pressures, indigenous groups have a set of tools to use in this circumstance. Many indigenous peoples have been generating tools for dealing with outsiders since the time of European expansion. Indigenous groups can approach globalization processes with a unique understanding. The economic impact of globalization in indigenous peoples is not quantified in any research yet.

In chiefdoms the commoners contributed to a fund for the chief's "office" (Sahlins 1968). The chiefdoms operated a centralized, public economy (Sahlins 1968). Funds were collected for the funding of the chief and his advisors, and there was also a "collective pooling and reallocation of goods by powers-that-be, a process deserving its own name—*redistribution*" (Sahlins 1968:94). The system of redistribution reflects the communal nature of society, something that reifies the community as a collective. This economic system is reflective of the communal culture, and "redistribution is chieftainship said in economics" (Sahlins 1968:95). The chiefdom was not a utopia. When the chiefdom and its office grew too large, it became a drain on the resources. The leaders of overgrown chiefdoms were subject to overthrow. When commoners were oppressed by the burdens, overthrow movements aimed at toppling the unjust ruler, not the chiefdom system, were launched (Sahlins 1968). The result is a flux: chiefdoms grow and shrink as people collectively revolt against the large chiefdom that swallows up resources (Sahlins 1968). Then the broken chiefdom atomizes, and eventually the smaller groups will reunite and create a larger community again (Sahlins 1968).

This is the economic and political system that was in place upon Captain Cook's arrival in the Hawaiian Island chain. This voyage introduced Hawai'i to the global economy, and thus globalization is not new. The Hawaiian chiefdoms left a legacy of "oppression and exploitation of maka'ainana (commoners) go as far back as the early traders" (Aoudé 1999:287). Hawaiian commoners had some freedoms, but as the laborers in the system of the chiefdom, they bore a great burden. Capitalism is blamed for the social ills that plague the Hawaiian Islands and the indigenous Hawaiians in the present day (Aoudé 2001). The Great *Mahele* of 1848 brought the shift towards capitalism, with private landholding. Capitalism was imposed on the islands, first via the "haole oligarchy and more recently, through a multi-ethnic (through primarily haole) bourgeoisie tied, as it is, to national and international capital" (Aoudé 1999:287). The capitalist class in Hawai'i was once part of the internationalist class, and is now part of the transnational capitalist class.

The state of Hawai'i has struggled with the economy in recent years. The economy is dominated by the tourism industry, which experienced losses during the minor American recession, and then the Asian financial crisis of the 1990's. The industry has not rebounded from these shocks, and continues to be vulnerable. The government's initial responses, aimed at diversification of the economy resulted in policies cultivating new tourist markets (Aoudé 1999). More recently, steps have been taken to promote industries such as biotechnology, information technology, communication services, health service, and medical research (Aoudé 2001). There is continued interest in promoting the tourism industry. All of this has been done with cooperation from the public and private sectors. The state is very aware of the global nature of the economy, and there is a keen awareness that Hawaiian workers are threatened by national and international capital, similar to workers in other locales (Aoudé 1999).

THE HAWAIIAN RENAISSANCE TO PRESENT DAY

Under territorial government, Native Hawaiians were encouraged to become American (Dudley and Agard 1993). Many adopted American ways as evidenced by the proliferation of the English Language, American media, and American schools contributed to the assimilation efforts (Dudley and Agard 1993). At the same time, Hawaiians and Hawaiian ways were stigmatized, exoticized, and eroticized (Trask, H. 1999). This was a part of the colonization and racialization of Hawaiians.³

In 1959, statehood comes for Hawai'i. The president signed the act granting statehood to Hawai'i on 18 March. In the proceedings that led to statehood, the Native Hawaiians were not asked for their consent (Dudley and Agard 1993). Instead, they were given two choices: statehood or remain a U.S. territory. With statehood, the United States quietly asked for Hawai'i to be removed from the United Nations' list of non-self-governing territories (Dudley and Agard 1993). Hawai'i was removed, and the privileges accorded to non-self-governing peoples were taken from the Native Hawaiians. In 1960 the state of Hawai'i held its first legislative session.

The early 1970s brought the beginning of the Hawaiian Renaissance. John Dominis Holt's *On Being Hawaiian* is credited with sparking the Renaissance (Dudley and Agard 1993). Prior to the renaissance, Native Hawaiians were "preoccupied with the efforts to succeed economically in the changing times, many parents told the Hawaiian kids to let go of the past and to adopt to changing ways" (Maunupau 1994:47). Holt wrote about the beauty of being Hawaiian, dispelling the negative stereotypes. The renaissance brought renewal of arts, crafts and music—and spread into the college classroom to include courses on Native Hawaiian knowledge and life (Dudley and Agard 1993). Hawaiian pride reemerged. The number of Hawaiian elected officials also rose with the Hawaiian Renaissance (Trask, H. 1999).

Calls for greater rights for Hawaiians within the state initially came from rural areas, where land struggles took the form of Native assertions of a birthright to the land and sea (Trask, H. 1999). Protests against eviction and other land struggles were the early expressions of the Hawaiian Movement. Anti-development battles responded to the growth of residential development and the resort industries. Kōkua Kalama protested housing developments and evictions unsuccessfully in the Kalama valley, but they inspired social activism and self-determination among the Hawaiians (Dudley and Agard 1993). Hawaiians occupied land and resisted evictions, demonstrated, took legal action, and participated in cultural assertion events (i.e. the construction of fishing villages) (Trask, H. 1999). Land struggles were against developers, and Hawaiian and non-Hawaiian locals fought together (Trask, H. 1999). With time, the Hawaiians began to separate themselves, and their claims became grounded in historical and cultural assertions specific to Native Hawaiians.

Native Hawaiians did not initially support the protests of development or evictions. They viewed their peers as radical and shameful (Dudley and Agard 1993). But with the incidents evicting the "beach people," views changed (Dudley and Agard 1993). Many of the evicted families moved to the beaches. Rents rose so much that they could not afford housing once they lost their homes. The "beach people" were a problem in the eyes of the state, which worried they would hurt the tourist industry. So, the "beach people" were evicted. Adults arrested for trespassing and images of the arrests and the crying children were on the evening news (Dudley and Agard 1993). These images galvanized the Hawaiians.

Defendants in eviction arrests began using sovereignty as theories of defense in trials (Trask, H. 1999). Nixon formally changed the policy towards U.S. indigenous Nations in the 1970's: from wardship to self-determination (Trask, H. 1999). This shift in policy makes their case stronger. Movement organizations sought to attain a land base, using legal corporations, political groups, and community coalitions to argue for reparations. Hawaiians need land to survive: "in the world view they developed in ancient days, islanders were participants along with the surrounding world of nature in a conscious, interrelating, familial community" (Dudley and Agard 1993: 82). Cooper (n. d.) calls land the engine of sovereignty. Self-government became the priority for Hawaiians. Initially these arguments were based upon wrongs done to Hawaiians in the process of annexation and statehood—the taking of nearly two million acres of trust lands according to one claim (Trask, H. 1999). The argument shifted to one rooted in aboriginal rights at a later time. For the Native Hawaiian movement, their claims as first and original claimants became crucial (Trask, H. 1999).

In the early 1970s, "local" referred to Hawaiian and non-Hawaiian residents of the islands (Trask, H. 1994 [1992]). Towards the end of the 1970s, indigenous Hawaiians began to assert their rights as unique from the rights of immigrants to Hawai'i (Trask, H. 1994 [1992]). The year 1978 marked the bicentennial of James Cook's arrival. Meanwhile the Hawaiian sovereignty movement was evolving. The focus of the movement shifted from restitution in the 1970s to sovereignty in the 1980s. Sovereignty came to be identified with statehood in the late 1980s (Trask, H. 1999). Native Hawaiians protested other events on the islands as well. Protesters spoke out against the drilling of thermal wells into Kīlauea, the taking of Homelands to build a spaceport, and the moving of graves on Maui (Dudley and Agard 1993). Protest did not mean greater opportunity for Native Hawaiians. "Hawai'i may have prospered since 1983, but not the Hawaiians" (Heckathorn 1998 [1992]: 343). In the early 1990s, Japanese investors owned sixty-five percent of the hotels on the Hawaiian Islands (Kelly 1994).

The year 1993, the 100th anniversary of the overthrow, was an eventful one in Hawai'i. The President of United Church of Christ apologized for the church's role in the overthrow. The U.S. Senate also apologized, and President Clinton signed a Congressional Resolution acknowledging the illegality of the overthrow. The Peoples' International Tribunal Hawai'i was hosted on the islands in 1993. This event linked indigenous peoples movements worldwide. The tribunal found multiple violations committed by the Untied States starting in 1790 through the present day (Peoples' International Tribunal Hawai'i 1994). These findings might be useful to the Hawaiian sovereignty movement community.

Hawaiians come in all shapes and sizes: wealthy, totally assimilated, those who are Hawaiian when it is convenient, Hawaiians who believe they are one group out of many on the islands, and those that don't support the sovereignty movement (Heckathorn 1998 [1988]). Native Hawaiians are a diverse populace in ancestry, traditional "Hawaiianness" in thought and behavior, religious attitudes and political views, health needs, Western educational and economic status, and in their family relations (Blaisdell and Mokuau 1994). Some Native Hawaiians are assimilated, and others are pluralists or nationalists (Blaisdell and Mokuau 1994). There is a small middle class of Hawaiians (Trask, H. 1994 [1992]). Otherwise, Hawaiians generally have high rates of: unemployment, catastrophic illness, institutionalization in the military or prisons, occupational ghettoization in poorly paid jobs, out migration that amounts to Diaspora, and low levels of educational attainment (Blaisdell and Mokuau 1994; Trask, H. 1994 [1992]). The Native Hawaiians became diasporized over the course of time. This happened relatively late as Native Hawaiians migrated to California and other western states. The Native Hawaiians who do not live on the islands continue to feel a tie to the land, a sense of place that is a part of their lives.

The Hawaiian sovereignty movement hinges on a few key historical events. These are the overthrow of the Hawaiian government in 1893, the 1898 annexation of the Hawaiian Islands by the United States, the 1959 plebiscite that granted Hawai'i status as the 50th state of the United States, and a 1993 bill that issued an apology for the 1893 overthrow and subsequent acts by the United States government. The acts making Hawai'i first a territory and then a state of the United States lack validity. By incorporating Hawai'i, the United States violated treaties and international law (Castanha 1996). The relationship between Hawaiians and the United States is an ongoing colonial relationship (Trask, H. 1999).

In general, Hawaiians seek a land base, land and financial restitution, access to native trust lands, and the protection of lands now being used by the United States military (Trask, H. 1999). There are three ways that sovereignty can be operationalized: complete separation from the United States as an independent and internationally recognized Hawai'i; existing as a Nation within a state, status with federal recognition akin to the experience of American Indian tribes; or maintaining the political status quo while working for reparations, control of Hawaiian trust assets by Hawaiians, and other freedoms (Hartwell 1996). Dudley and Agard (1993) include three other options: Nation-to-Nation status,[4] following the example of the Iroquois relationship with the United States government; creating a sovereign territory on the ceded lands or contiguous lands swapped for the ceded lands; or taking a few islands for the sovereign Nation and leaving the rest as a part of the United States. Each expression of sovereignty grants Hawaiians the right to reshape their political and social experience. Native Hawaiians recognize that creating a Hawaiian nation in the islands will be a challenge to non-Hawaiians, even though their plans do not include taking private property or evicting non-Hawaiians (Heckathorn 1998 [1988]).

If Hawai'i were able to attain independence, citizenship would be available to non-Hawaiians. Hawai'i would have the power to limit immigration, design foreign policy, and establish its own trade agreements. The citizens would have the power to determine the form of government, perhaps including traditional elements. The United States military bases would be closed. Under the Nation within a Nation model, Hawaiian sovereignty would consist of self-government for Native Hawaiians while they remain citizens of the United States. Native Hawaiians would manage Hawaiian lands and assets (Hartwell 1996). A Hawaiian legislature would make laws and oversee the use of Hawaiian homelands.

While reverse discrimination lawsuits are spreading in the continental United States, the same sentiment has grown in Hawai'i. As Hawaiians struggle to assert their rights as a Nation, they must also guard the rights given by the state of Hawai'i. Two lawsuits risk special rights due to Native Hawaiians from the Office of Hawaiian Affairs. Both lawsuits argue that rights given to Native Hawaiians by the state of Hawai'i discriminate against non-Native Hawaiians. Rice v. Ceytano argues that non-Hawaiians should be allowed to vote for members of the Board of Trustees of the Office of Hawaiian Affairs, and that to prohibit non-natives from participating was discriminatory. The judge agreed. The other case is still being heard. Barrett is the plaintiff in this case, and he argues that the Office of Hawaiian Affairs is discriminatory because it serves only Native Hawaiians. These two lawsuits could implicitly render the Office of Hawaiian Affairs unable to serve the needs of Native Hawaiians. If this does happen,

Hawaiians will be even further limited in their ability to seek special status as indigenous Nations within the United States government.

SOVEREIGNTY MOVEMENT ORGANIZATIONS

The Hawaiian Renaissance motivated the return to culture, language, arts, and crafts. Sovereignty[5] movements began to form, following the land rights movements, in the 1970s. There are multiple movement organizations seeking different forms of sovereignty (Trask, H. 1999). Some of them have longer histories than others. The organizations sought to attain a land base, using legal corporations, political groups, and community coalitions to argue for reparations. Initially these arguments were based upon wrongs done to Hawaiians, then the argument shifted to one rooted in aboriginal rights.

A significant time for all of the sovereignty movement organizations was August 1988, when a Native Hawaiian Rights Conference was held. Charles F. Wilkinson was a speaker, and motivated Native Hawaiians to seek their right to self-determination. At this conference, the sovereignty groups agreed to speak with a united voice of the need for sovereignty, but maintain the different organizations in order to generate a greater diversity of ideas and strategies (Dudley and Agard 1993). This fluidity also allows for a uniform voice that can prevent the groups from splintering over small details that are not relevant at this time (e.g. concrete details about how the Nation might be governed if it were to achieve sovereignty).

The Hawaiian Nation has a longstanding goal of achieving sovereignty. "Native Hawaiians never abandoned their quest to regain sovereignty and reestablish their nation" (Trask, M. 1994:79). Surveys suggest that interest in Hawaiian sovereignty may be ebbing among the general Native Hawaiian population (Office of Hawaiian Affairs). Still, this might be due to the fact that other issues have risen and are demanding priority.[6] The organizations are seeking self-sufficiency as a goal they can achieve in nationhood (Trask, M. 1994). Land is also central in the fight: "the act admitting Hawai'i to statehood in 1959 obligated the state to hold the lands entrusted to it and the income from them as a public trust" (Getches et al 1993: 950). Generally speaking, sovereignty movement organizations seek self-government over reparations (Trask, H. 1994 [1992]). The sovereignty coalition, Hui Na'auao, consisted of forty organizations as of 1998 (Heckathorn). I will briefly describe a handful of these organizations and their goals below.

A group called The Hawaiians organized in 1970 to seek reforms in the Hawaiian Homelands program and the Bishop Estate (Castanha

1996). In 1972, the group called A.L.O.H.A. formed. A.L.O.H.A. stands for Aboriginal Lands of Hawaiian Ancestry, and is inspired by the Queen's autobiography and the passing of the Alaska Native Claims Settlement Act in 1971 (Dudley and Agard 1993). The organization raised money and hired a former congressman to draw up a bill for reparations for Hawaiians (Dudley and Agard 1993). The bill was never ratified, but congress did respond by setting up a study commission. The commission had only six months to do research, and relied upon biased sources for information: work by the author commissioned to write textbooks on Hawaiian history by the territorial government and United States Navy historians (Dudley and Agard 1993). The commission recommended against reparations, and A.L.O.H.A. wrote a strong dissenting paper (Dudley and Agard 1993).

In 1973, three new organizations emerged: The Homerule Movement, the Hawaiian Coalition, and Hui Malama 'Aina O Ko'olau (Castanha 1996). 'Ohana O Hawai'i formed in 1974. This group seeks sovereignty for Hawaiian people. They argue that the Queen may have abdicated her throne, but the people of Hawai'i did not surrender their sovereignty (Dudley and Agard 1993). This organization has taken Hawai'i's case to the World Court at The Hague and other international tribunals (Dudley and Agard 1993). Other sovereignty movements were born in 1974. These include the Council of Hawaiian Organizations, Alu Like, and the Native Hawaiian Legal Corporation (Castanha 1996). The Native Hawaiian Legal Corporation is still active. It is a non-profit law firm active in representing Native clients in land claims cases and also works for sovereignty.

Protect Kaho'olawe 'Ohana (P.K.O.) formed in the mid 1970's, with members of A.L.O.H.A. and Hui Ala Loa, to seek the repatriation of the island of Kaho'olawe (Dudley and Agard 1993). Protect Kaho'olawe 'Ohana supports decentralized island based autonomous entities (Trask, H. 1999).

More movements were born in 1975. Hui Ala Loa was formed on Molokai and Hou Hawaiians formed to seek federal recognition from the federal government (Castanha 1996). Under this status, Native Hawaiians would have the same political status as American Indians. The Institute for the Advancement of Hawaiian Affairs organization, known as the Sovereignty for Hawai'i Committee, was created in 1985 (Castanha 1996). The Institute for the Advancement of Hawaiian Affairs supports secession (Trask, H. 1999).

An informal group of people occupied Anahola Beach Park beginning in 1986 (Field-Grace 1994). They built a traditional village site, which they named 'Ili Noho Kai O Anahola (the Anahola District by the Sea). The state evicted the individuals occupying the site and the National Guard destroyed the homes, gardens, and any other improvements while the occupants were on trial (Field-Grace 1994). The occupants returned and were arrested and released again. They rebuilt again and as of January 1993 the village was still in existence (Field-Grace 1994).

Ka Pakuakau was founded in 1989. Hui Na'auao formed in 1991. This is a coalition of 47 groups focusing on sovereignty education (Castanha 1996). Nā ʻŌiwi o Hawai'i seeks sovereignty, but supports community education before a mechanism for government is established (Trask, H. 1999). E Ola Mau is a group of health professionals in support of the decentralized island based entities (Trask, H. 1999). An organization called The Pro-Hawaiian Sovereignty Working Group, consisting of professors, doctors, lawyers, and activists, publishes a regular newsletter on the sovereignty movement (Dudley and Agard 1993). Education on sovereignty and the issues surrounding it are essential.

The Council of Hawaiian Organizations supports a constitutionally established political body on a separate land base (Trask, H. 1999). In the year 1992, two organizations formed: the restored Kingdom of Hawai'i and the 'Ohana Council of the Hawaiian Kingdom, now known as the Sovereign Nation-State of Hawai'i or the Nation of Hawai'i (Castanha 1996). The Hawaiian Nation seeks: no submission to Jurisdiction, proper alignment of parties, diminished status of commission, no extinguishment of the right to self-determination (Ka Pae'aina o Hawai'i Loa (United Independence Statement) 1999). The Nation of Hawai'i declared independence in 1994 in a response to the 1993 Public Law 103–150, the apology bill (Castanha 1996). At the same time a handful of other sovereignty organizations called for independence, including Ka Pakuakau, the Institute for the Advancement of Hawaiian Affairs, 'Ohana O Hawai'i, and the Kingdom of Hawai'i (Castanha 1996).

Ka Lāhui Hawai'i formed in 1987 and argues for the inclusion of Hawaiians in federal Indian policy, sovereignty, and nationhood (this term came to be used as of 1988) (Trask, H. 1999). The arguments stem from "the culpability of the United States in the loss of Hawaiian domain and dominion in 1893, the unilateral change in Native citizenship that came with forcible annexation in 1898, and the internationally recognized right of all peoples to self-determination" (Trask, H. 1999:71). Ka Lāhui Hawai'i seeks federal recognition of Hawaiians as a Native Nation with all of the rights extended to Indian Nations on the mainland (Trask, H. 1999). The organization has five stated goals to achieve reconciliation: resolution of historic claims related to the overthrow, misuse to native trust lands, violation of human and civil rights, and federally held lands and resources; an end to U.S. policy not recognizing Native Hawaiian sovereignty—

including an end to the wardship status; recognition of Ka Lāhui as a Hawaiian Nation (including jurisdiction over national assets, lands and natural resources); commitment to decolonize Hawai'i via United Nations process for non-self-governing territories; and finally the restoration of traditional lands, national resources, ocean and energy resources to the Ka Lāhui National Land Trust (Trask, H. 1999). Ka Lāhui Hawai'i has written a constitution with four arms of government: executive, legislative, judicial, and *ali'i nui* (high chief) (Dudley and Agard 1993).

The state legislature and governor supported sovereignty as of 1993, forming and funding the Hawaiian Sovereignty Advisory Council (Dudley and Agard 1993). This organization was created to study Hawaiian nationhood and consists of eleven grass-roots organizations and state agencies (Dudley and Agard 1993). This organization is now known as the Hawaiian Sovereignty Election Council, and its job is to determine the will of Native Hawaiian people regarding sovereignty (Castanha 1996). They held a plebiscite, asking the question "Shall the Hawaiian people elect delegates to propose a Native Hawaiian government?" (as quoted in Castanha 1996). The plebiscite failed, and was critiqued across the Hawaiian Nation. Some felt the plebiscite was rushed; others felt that there was not enough education on the issue (Castanha 1996). Another criticism questions the role of a state organization in overseeing the formation of an independent Hawai'i (Castanha 1996). The conflict of interest is clear.

Office of Hawaiian Affairs (OHA) was created in 1978 to represent Hawaiian rights (Trask, H. 1999). Much like the Bureau of Indian Affairs, this office has been plagued with problems: it is powerless to control trust lands, has no statutory strength to protect Hawaiian culture, trustees are unpaid and turnover is high, misuse of OHA monies by heads of the board (twice), sex scandals, mismanagement of funds, and misrepresented programs to the state legislature (Trask, H. 1999). OHA attempted to assert itself as the governing body over Hawaiians in the late 1980's. This was too much of a conflict of interest: OHA was a state agency and as such Hawaiian money would go through the state, and giving the OHA Nation status would be erroneous—as much as giving the BIA Nation status would be (Trask, H. 1999). The OHA is mired in controversy: it has a collaborative relationship with the Democratic Party, a conflict of interest as an organization funded by the state which is supposed to serve the Native Hawaiians, and a history of supporting destructive developments (Trask, H. 1999).

At the Hawaiian Rights Conference (in 1988) with OHA and Hawaiian leaders, the community came up a five-plank[7] plan designed to grant Hawaiians the freedoms they seek. Following this meeting the OHA drew up conditions for reparations in 1989. The reparations plan was flawed: it lacked a plan for the inclusion of Hawaiians in federal Indian policy, made no claims against the state in spite of a record of mismanaged trust lands, and OHA would control all Hawaiian assets (Trask, H. 1999). The OHA and the governor reached an agreement for reparations in 1990. The result was another loss of land: the state paid $100 million in 1991 and $8.5 million every subsequent year for 1.5 million acres of ceded lands (Trask, H. 1999). This was not a win in the eyes of many Hawaiians, who saw that money was at the center of this settlement, and not land (Trask, H. 1999). With this settlement in 1991 came a continued status for Native Hawaiians as wards of the state. Sovereignty groups must work independently of OHA if they do not wish to be intrinsically linked to the State of Hawai´i.

SPECTRUM OF SOVEREIGNTY

Globalization has not fundamentally changed sovereignty: findings that suggest otherwise are relying upon the existence of an imaginary past in which sovereignty holds exaggerated significance (Krasner 1999). It is important to realize this in a setting of globalization, which is bringing rapid change on a global scale to all social institutions. A sociological study of sovereignty should be two-pronged, to include analysis and development (Commons 1988). In the process of analysis, the sociologist considers the qualities of the sovereign body, and its relations with other organizations and institutions, focusing on the concept of sovereignty (Commons 1899). In looking at development, a sociologist ought to trace the formation of sovereignty and the State (Commons 1899). Although Commons limits sovereignty to the study of the State, the concept does apply to other political bodies. The sociological study of sovereignty can consider sub-state or super-state organizations, such as the United Nations, the European Union, an American Indian tribe or band (e.g. the Yakama Tribe), or the Native Hawaiians.

Generally speaking, sovereignty provides protections from interference with rights and freedoms. Sovereignty can be expressed in many different forms, along a spectrum ranging from a new independent State to rights of free cultural expression within the existing State. The form and degree of autonomy are matters for negotiation between the Nation and the State authorities. The shape of a spectrum is useful because it can indicate the positioning of a country in terms of high or low levels of sovereignty. There is a great deal of gray in the middle where it might be difficult to say which group is more or less sovereign, and the spectrum allows for this too.

The Native Hawaiians in their present situation are on the lower end of the spectrum of sovereignty. Native Hawaiians have the freedom to engage in cultural practices, and their language is enjoying a resurgence. They have some ability to govern themselves via the Office of Hawaiian Affairs (OHA), but this right is eroded by a lawsuit allowing non-Native Hawaiians to vote for OHA board members. Towards the middle of the spectrum are the American Indians, the Welsh, the Nunavut, and the Scottish. According to the Marshall Decision in the 1830's, American Indian tribes are domestic independent Nations with the power to govern within the reservations only (Cooper n.d.). In 1997 there was a vote to reestablish the Welsh Assembly, and just prior to the vote the Welsh were given representation in the European Union. A 1993 plebiscite resulted in creation of Nunavut territory, a large section of the Northern Territories carved out for indigenous peoples, in April of 1999. In 1997 there was a vote to reestablish the Scottish Parliament, and the Parliament was granted tax-varying power. It has also been suggested that Scottish parliament needs to represent Scottish interests in the United Kingdom and in Brussels. At the most extreme high end of the spectrum of operationalization of sovereignty is exemplified by the plans of Ka Lāhui Hawai'i. In their vision, the Native Hawaiian sovereignty movement will culminate in an independent State with a government consisting of four branches (executive, legislative, judicial, and *ali'i nui*).

These examples are illustrative of the varying manners of operationalizing sovereignty. There are countless ways for a community to express sovereignty: ability to develop independent political institutions; determining the form of their government; the ability to participate in government at all levels; communal or collective property rights; right to harvest natural resources, fish or game; and the right to regulate industrial or other development on aboriginal lands. It is not for international law to prescribe the precise form that sovereignty can take.

CONCLUSION

Hawai'i is an island state in the United States with a fragile environment and a thriving tourist industry. There are contradictions in the needs of the environment and the needs of the economy, in the needs of the native peoples and the needs of the capitalists. The islands have developed a welcoming and open culture, exhibiting the indigenous arts, dance, and music. Yet the people sharing their culture are among the most poor on the islands. Native Hawaiians also have higher rates of alcoholism, infant mortality, incarceration, suicide, and high school dropouts. The welcoming culture clashes with the economic, social, and political realities of the Native Hawaiian experience. The population is problematized and romanticized, but not realized.

The experience of being colonized by outsiders changed the Hawaiians. Being colonized is an invasion. As a result of the colonial experience, lands were stolen, cultures were assimilated, the language was nearly lost, the right to self-govern was taken, and people now live in the shadow of what they once were. The case of Native Hawai'i exemplifies one of the greatest losses at the hands of a powerful, external State.

The history of Hawaiian activism goes back to the beginning of American intrusion in Hawaiian government and politics. Before the United States annexed Hawai'i, treaties negotiated with foreign countries asserted Hawaiian independence. Once American political power asserted itself as the dominant one in the islands, Hawaiians inserted themselves in the American political construct, building a Democratic Party membership organization (Trask, H. 1999). Through the Democratic Party, Hawaiians worked to promote the inclusion of Hawai'i in the union, believing that statehood would give them more power than the territorial political structure. Hawaiians have experienced ups and downs over the course of the state history, and now seek self-government to end the ongoing colonial relationship.

The Hawaiian Renaissance is growing and the culture is reviving. The Hawaiian sovereignty movement is gaining new audiences with the Internet, the United Nations, and by joining with other indigenous peoples. They are adopting the languages of human rights and freedom, putting a new twist on old claims. Claims for rights to tribal traditions (i.e. worship at Kaho'olawe), and claims for land and water rights are placing a wedge in the door to freedoms. The new audience and the new language are allowing the Native Hawaiians to better articulate their situation, and it is also allowing them to be better understood.

The Hawaiian Kingdom has a constitution, a queen, and an envoy to the United Nations. Legally, the claim for Hawaiian sovereignty is strong, and the Hawaiian Nation uses these symbols to their advantage to mobilize the Native Hawaiian population. Many Hawaiians believe that under the United States government, they "are not now autonomous yet dependent. Rather, we are dependent *and* subjugated" (Trask, H. 1999: 103). Sovereignty is one solution. If the end result is not sovereignty, the Hawaiians will not be losers if they have maintained their solidarity. Sovereignty is something to work towards, but the community vision for self-government must be one of unity.

Chapter Five
Global, Local, and/or Hybrid Identities

The individual or community with a hybrid identity mimics the result of globalization: the squeezing of the world community with a simultaneous expansion of the world community. Hybridity[1] has become one way to re-create and re-vision a community, while incorporating elements of outside groups. A hybrid identity forms when elements of two or more cultures are merged and thereby create a new cultural identity. The hybrid occupies partial identities, multiple roles, and pluralistic selves.

Initially hybridity was a term of derision, often as a mixed-blood or genetic reference. DuBois (1996 [1903]) describes the negative experience of African Americans, attempting to occupy this space that is in between: being insiders and outsiders at the same time. The individual who wears this title can never be entirely included, and is always a stranger. As a boy DuBois asks himself "why did God make me an outcast and a stranger in mine own house?" (1996 [1903]). The hybrid space can be a cause of internal strife. There is a negative connotation in being an outsider. But, with globalization and increasing modernization, being a hybrid is now a benefit. The ability to negotiate across barriers: language, cultural, spiritual, racial, and physical; is an asset. Those who can easily cross barriers in a world of amorphous borders have an advantage.

Indigenous Nations have been developing and adopting hybrid identities since colonialism began. They have the ability to interact with outsiders and have managed to maintain their cultural integrity at the same time. Hybridity presents several options for indigenous Nations as they position themselves vis-à-vis the State. State bodies, which work under the logic of commerce and military, are self-contained. Indigenous Nations are involved in the globalizing process. They respond to the changes with evolution. States respond to the changes with fortified borders.

This chapter considers collective cultural identity. To contextualize the discussion, I consider internal colonialism and globalization first. Then I define the global, local, and hybrid identity types. This is followed by examples from the Native Hawaiian case. Prior to the conclusion, I talk about the expression of hybridity in interactions with the State.

AN INTERNAL COLONY EXPERIENCE

One result of State building was the increased importance of borders. Compared to the geography of empires, known for their strings of outposts that defined the territorial expanse of power, State boundaries were new. State political bodies control bounded territories. States created or extended borders by patterns of linguistic similarity, or the presence of a physical boundary (Poggi 1978). The social relations of the State were conducted over space, a social construct (Massey 1985). State boundaries were partially related to population patterns, but this was not the main force in establishing borders. While indigenous Nations remained, State borders shifted and solidified around them. For indigenous Nations, ties to the land are strong, and are both tangible and intangible. A group may need access to natural resources on the land, or it may have religious ties to a specific location. By establishing historical roots to a physical territory, they provide evidence of their identity and culture. The shifting of the political borders brings a shift to the social relations within the space for the indigenous and the new State.

The idea of internal colonialism comes from the power-conflict school of theory, which emphasizes the role of stratification and power. Internal colonialism debunks the salt-water thesis, which suggests that colonies can only exist overseas. An internal colony is a colony within the boundaries of the State that colonized it. This concept is significant because "by defining inter-regional relationships as 'colonial,' nationalist leaders have tried to inspire popular support for movements designed to promote greater autonomy, if not outright secession" (Stone 1996 [1979]: 279). Many American Indian Nations have been colonized more than once, initially by European powers (e.g. Great Britain, France, Spain), and now are internal colonies of the United States. Although Hawai'i was once a colony under the saltwater thesis, as the United States absorbed the islands it became an internal colony. The internal colony is subjected to oppression from the outside government, questions of legitimacy, and forced assimilation. The colonizing government legitimates their expropriations by transposing them into "customs," but the indigenous can appeal to the same customs they resist.

The experience of indigenous Nations is unique in several ways. Unlike immigrants, they did not choose to be in a new situation. Instead it developed around them. Unlike Diasporas, they have maintained ties to their locality. Some indigenous Nations have begun to diasporize, but this is relatively recent and is sometimes due to the force of State policy. As internal colonies, indigenous Nations are a society living within another society. They live under legal rules and cultural norms of the external society most of the time, simultaneously seeking to maintain cultural and legal independence and integrity. Instead of embracing new cultures and appreciating the new horizons, as immigrants to new States might do, indigenous Nations labor to maintain the integrity of their own culture while learning to exist within the setting created by the outsiders.

THE CREOLE HYBRID

A Creole is a person born of European ancestry who is born outside of Europe, such as in the Americas, Africa, or Asia. (Anderson 1991: 47n). These people occupy a unique place in relations to the colonial power and the colony. This is another type of hybrid, as the person of European descent gradually incorporates elements of the local culture, leading to the creation of a new identity. The Creole is European by birth, and European *and* colonial in culture. Like the African American, two separate identities exist within the one person, labeled a Creole. Similar to the American Indian, this person is struggling to maintain a traditional identity, European, while living within a foreign community, the American, African, or Asian colony. The Creole is a hybrid identity that emerged in the early days of European expansion around the globe.

GLOBALIZATION

Globalization is a set of processes resulting in a shrinking of the globe and the proliferation of the idea that we live in one world. Indicators of globalization are moving around the world in an uneven pattern (Giddens 2000:34). This is a truly global shift in the economy, politics, and society. The process of globalization has a long history, beginning with: "the acquisition of a world view by Europeans [which] produced as its long-term outcome the world's first truly global culture" (Spybey 1996:1). The global economy is changing as the spread of globalization changes consumers, markets, and the conditions of industry. People are standardized as technology spreads and they become mass consumers, skilled laborers, and users of common communications networks. Globalization is simultaneously characterized as the only avenue to world prosperity and the greatest threat to human development (Cheru 2000).

The processes of globalization are contradictory: it promotes and inhibits democracy, is homogenizing and diversifying, standardizing and localizing (Kellner 2002). The structural aspects of globalization include the economy, communication, the military, and the State system (Spybey 1996). Beck (2000) defines globalization as "the *process* through which sovereign National States are criss-crossed and undermined by transnational actors with varying prospects of power, orientations, identities and networks" (11). Transnational, not international, agents are playing key roles in the globalization of politics, the economy, and culture. Globalization is remarkable for its scope and its depth, "with increasing intensity *inside* nationally constituted societies" (Robertson 1992: 104). To summarize, globalization is a set of processes that are moving around the globe, re-shaping economic systems, political bodies, and cultural identities. The result is a combination of standardization, specification, and hybridization, which incorporates local knowledge and the new cosmopolitanism.

In a globalized society, it is difficult to conceptualize the State society independent of the exterior influences (Hall 1997). Regions are being squeezed together in new ways. These conditions can destabilize the State and the State system. To maintain its relevance and power, the State must be active in political, social, and economic institutions (Griffin 2000). With globalization, "democracy spreads and more political regions and spaces of everyday life are being contested by democratic demands and forces" (Kellner 2002:292). New bodies are forming, following the shape of a democratic political system at international and regional levels—including sub-state and super-state regions. For the State to remain a part of the global political system, it must adapt to the new conditions (Griffin 2000). This is a dynamic political environment that must be carefully navigated for the good of the State and the citizenry.

The pressures of globalization produce a shift to cosmopolitanism *and* localism. A time/space compression is acting to both unite and divide communities socially (Bauman 1998). Media and migration allow for imaginations to be more expanded than ever before. People share the experiences of globetrotting friends; enjoy international foods and entertainment, and witness events around the globe via the media (Appadurai 1998). They are cosmopolitans. Communications allow people to be transnational citizens. The standardization of technologies and goods means that people on opposite sides of the world might be wearing the same clothing or watching the same television programs. This challenges the maintenance of group identity: "standard cultural reproduction is now an endangered activity" (Appadurai 1998:54). Yet, cultures and communities are finding new ways to survive and thrive. In many cases, globalization processes are answered with localization (Beck 2000, Giddens 2000). Local groups are strengthening and redefining themselves, as globalization encourages the reemergence of localization. Societies are exposed to outside influences, which results in a community "characterized by frayed edges and loose textures" (Oommen 1998: 238). Along the frayed edges hybrid cultural identities are emerging, which are distinct combinations of global cosmopolitanism and local cultures.

There has been a global economy since colonization began, which was partially driven by economic interests. Consumption and production are global. Capital and trade are now transnational, and transnational corporations are replacing multi-national corporations (Aoudé 2001). The core dominates world production and trade. Globalization has given rise to a transnational capitalist class, a transnational working class, and a transnational State (Aoudé 2001). The manufacture of goods is globalized. Corporations establish factories where environmental protections and tariffs are minimal and cheap laborers are plentiful. In the interdependent global economy, there is minimal local autonomy (Spybey 1996). Wages are rising and falling everywhere and workers are losing control over their labor markets and terms of employment (Greider 1997). They are losing control because businesses can easily shift to a "friendlier" locale, one that is less controversial in terms of labor rights or environmental rights or can offer lower levels of taxation.

Some communities experience rising oppression as a result of globalizing markets. International trade is not automatically equalized by the removal of barriers. Instead, wage-price differences between countries render free-trade unequal (Tabb 2002; Kohler 2003). Free trade generates income and redistributes it. Some gain in the redistribution, and some lose. Sustainable development programs are a means of protecting the poor (Falk 2000). Yet, thus far the funds set aside for such policies have been inadequate, and there are serious questions about the investment—financial and otherwise—in sustainable development (Falk 2000). Globalization from above is limited in its capacity to create equality (Cheru 2000:122). In the global spread of capitalism, "the poor, who have few choices, may sell the very space they occupy for short-term reward" (Tabb 2002:50). Capitalism is an economic theory based on the logical pursuit of profits—it is incompatible with social justice, or an egalitarian perspective. Yet as global communication rises, new bonds of solidarity are forming and awareness of oppression is growing, which creates more opportunity for change.

GLOBAL, LOCAL, AND HYBRID IDENTITY TYPES

Imagined communities conceive of elements of culture and tradition as being local, for example traditional diet and language—especially slang; or global, for example McDonalds and Ford cars. Yet, the hybrid and the global are more difficult to distinguish. In many ways, the idea of one global identity might be the equivalent of a generalized hybrid identity. For the purposes of this paper, I must draw a line between these two concepts. Hybrid identities emerge that are unique because of the local context (Spybey 1996). To an outsider the distinction might seem like splitting hairs. But for members of the local community, the small differences can be considerable. The difference between a global identity and a hybrid identity is the variation that is due to the contextual characteristics. Everything has a context, and within this context the meaning is defined.

Global Identity

Border erosion that began with colonialism will continue as cultures experience more exposure to other cultures. Institutionalization, regulation, and economic rationalization promote the development of a universal identity (Wagner 2001). It is not surprising that a more standard culture follows the standardization of economic and political systems. The global culture is centered in the West, speaks English, and is a partial homogenization (Hall 1997). The media influences the global society (Appadurai 1998, Beck 2000). This is a dynamic culture. A global culture is "subject to a continuous interplay between its universal aspects and those of its particularistic reproduction" (Spybey 1996: 159). The global culture is constantly created and re-created. Although elements of the global culture have clear roots in the West, the global culture is not just a process of Westernization. This is because the global culture is reproduced reflexively: it varies by context (Spybey 1996). Local contexts adopt the global culture, and also contribute local elements to the global culture.

Local Identity

Local communities are fragile: producing and maintaining locality in the midst of the massive flows of information across the globe is difficult (Appadurai 1998). The local is bombarded with the global from all sides. One response to globalization is the reemergence of localization (Hall 1997; Giddens 2000). Communities respond to the stimulus with an eye to reinvigorating the local. Local culture has long been constrained, as it is reproduced within the context and constraints of the State. Local communities risk autonomy as they become "increasingly dependent on sense-giving and interpreting actions which they do not control" (Bauman 1998:3). Exposure to cosmopolitan media, language, and technology can risk the integrity of the local culture. As local communities are exposed to outside influences, the community can become increasingly amorphous. The local community must achieve a delicate balance between outside influence and internal distinction.

Hybridity

Hybridity results when two or more cultures are incorporated to create a new cultural identity. The identities are not assimilated or altered independently—bits of identities become elements of a new identity. A third identity emerges which is not the same as the independent parts. It is common to find hybridity in the context of a colonized culture that has been destabilized (Gandhi 1998). When cultures take in elements of global influence, they are doing so within the context of their local lives and creating a new hybrid. Individuals occupying a hybrid space simultaneously experience a doubleness and cultural intermixture (Gilroy 1993). Although the hybrid contains elements of the local and the global, the intermixture makes it unique. The hybrid concept has roots in the hard sciences (e.g. botany or biology), but also in the social sciences.

Simmel's (1950) study of "The Stranger" considers hybridity. The stranger arrives today and has the *potential* to leave tomorrow (Simmel 1950). Strangers are simultaneously members of the community and not members of the community. They are not seen as individuals, but as a particular type that is a combination of the stranger's identity and the local identity. One resolution to the problem of having two identities or being identified by types and labels is to create a new identity. DuBois (1996 [1903]) describes hybridity as resulting in a double consciousness. Groups that occupy this space experience a kind of "two-ness," as two identities trying to exist within one person (DuBois 1996 [1903]). Expanding this idea to all blacks in the West, Gilroy describes the position as "between (at least) two great cultural assemblages" (Gilroy 1993:1). The individual occupying a hybrid space navigates between two cultural groups, and occupies space within both cultural groups. This space holds a challenge and a privilege. The African American is described as having a veil, and a second sight (DuBois 1996 [1903]). The veil creates distance, but the second sight affords a way of seeing the self in the view of others.

Hybrid identities continue to be predominant in minority or immigrant communities, but these are not the only sites of hybridity in the globalized world. Hybridity takes place where communication, negotiation, and translation bridge societies, and a new political object forms (Bhabha

1994). Given a compressed world and a constrained State, identities for all individuals and collective selves are becoming more complex. The creation of a hybrid identity is a "twofold process involving *the interpenetration of the universalization of particularism and the particularization of universalism*" (Robertson 1992: 100). The local and the global interact to create a new identity that is distinct in each context. As the two interact, the local influences the global and the global influences the local. A reflexive relationship between the local and global produces the hybrid. The local is universalized and the universal is localized, resulting in a new hybrid. The result is a form of hybridity that "signifies the encounter, conflict, and/or blending of two ethnic or cultural categories which, while by no means pure and distinct in nature, tend to be understood and experienced as meaningful identity labels by members of these categories" (Lo 2002:199). This blending of multiple cultural categories is happening around the world, and hybrid identities are emerging.

As mentioned earlier, hybridity can also be interpreted in a biological sense, inspired by the study of plant life. Young's (1995) review of the genealogy of the term "hybrid" illustrates this. In the more literal interpretation, the hybrid is the product of "pure" or "distinct" categories. Notions of purity cannot be as easily linked to cultural identities, which consist of constructed and imagined elements. Cultures are not sealed off from each other (Gilroy 1993), which renders it nearly impossible to assert that there are "pure" cultures that could produce a hybrid—in this interpretation. In the plant world purity can be maintained with plastic bags and controlled pollination by a gardener. The same gardener can engineer hybrids, as Mendel illustrated with his peas, using planned cross-pollinating. Even the most isolated culture cannot be so carefully maintained or manipulated. Instead of using the more literal biological model, I choose to follow recent scholarship in postcolonial studies (as described in the paragraphs above). Biology is an excellent inspiration for the idea of the hybrid, but it does not properly reflect the process of cultural production.

CASE STUDY

Hawai'i is an island state in the United States with a fragile environment and a thriving tourist industry. There are contradictions in the needs of the environment and the needs of the economy, in the needs of the native Nation and the needs of the capitalists. The islands have developed a welcoming and open culture, exhibiting the indigenous arts, dance, and music. Yet the people sharing this culture are among the most poor on the islands. Native Hawaiians also have higher rates of alcoholism, infant mortality, incarceration, suicide, and high school dropouts. The welcoming culture clashes with the economic, social, and political realities of the Native Hawaiian experience. The population is problematized, romanticized, but not realized.

Below are examples from the contemporary Native Hawaiian experience. These outline examples of global, local, and hybrid identities that can be found in Native Hawaiian culture. It is not always possible to rely solely upon the author or speaker's assertion that: here is an example of local culture. This may not be overtly stated. I infer which category the examples fall under, using the author's tone, text, and sometimes reading between the lines. These examples illustrate the theoretical distinction between the types of cultural expression in one community. They offer empirical evidence to support the distinction that I establish above.

Examples of Global Identity

The traditional Native Hawaiian diet consists predominantly of *poi*, fish, sweet potato, squid, breadfruit, and other seafood and tropical fruits. Today, people tend to eat globally, including Western foods (e.g. soda, hamburgers, pizza) or Asian food (e.g. McDonalds restaurants in Hawai'i serve miso soup). Some Native Hawaiians still eat items unique to the traditional Native Hawaiian diet, but this is no longer the primary source of nutrition and sustenance. This is one way that Native Hawaiians, especially urban Native Hawaiians, are expressing a global identity.

Native Hawaiians are adopting global technologies and conveniences. The use of the internet to convey information about Native Hawaiian sovereignty movement activity, the Native Hawaiian government, and other local political and social issues (e.g. a discussion of a Hollywood movie chronicling the life of King Kamehameha and disputes about the actor selected to play the lead role) is one way that Native Hawaiians embrace a global technology and communication system. Native Hawaiians generally live in the modern technological world: they drive cars, have 9–5 jobs, and live in non-traditional homes.

Elements of Hawaiian culture have been co-opted by the global community. Native Hawaiian cultural practices are recognized around the world. The *lei*, *aloha*, *luau*, *hula*, surfing, the outrigger canoe, and carved wooden totems have become a part of the global society. Visitors travel to Hawai'i to "hang loose" and enjoy the island paradise. They are exposed to Hawaiian culture in commercialized Polynesian shows, *luaus*, and *hula* demonstrations sponsored by Kodak film. The Hawaiian culture is prostituted by the tourism industry—as it attracts visitors and revenue, it cheapens and devalues the culture (Trask, H. 1999). The strong local tradition is attractive to travelers. The attraction of large numbers of international visitors annually for vacations is evidence of its insertion into the global culture.

Examples of Local Identity

Hula remains a vibrant aspect of Hawaiian culture, with modern and ancient traditions still being practiced. Outside of the Polynesian shows popular with tourists, *hula* has a life with the locals. Annual competitions are held, and schools of *hula* teach dancers, prepare for competitions, and continue a unique aspect of Hawaiian culture. Through *hula* and *hula* lessons, students learn Hawaiian values and norms. They also learn a distinct form of communication and art. Teachers continue an ancient tradition while creating new elements of an old art form.

While many Hawaiian arts and crafts survived colonialism and modernization, others are at risk of being lost. *Kapa*, the weaving of fabric from bark, is one of these art forms. This craft is an especially demanding one because all of the tools must be handmade. The making of the tools is a part of the training in the craft of *kapa*. One man, Dennis Kana'e Keawe, a native revivalist, has acquired *kapa* making skills through research and practice (Hartwell 1996). By examining objects in museums and books, Keawe has learned the art of *kapa*, and other Hawaiian crafts such as weaving, feather capes, and drum making. In his work, Keawe uses natural materials harvested from the forests of the islands. Keawe is a member of a community of contemporary artisans who are self-taught or university trained. The Kamehameha schools and the University of Hawai'i, along with self-trained individuals, are working to rejuvenate a community of artisans that was lost during the colonial era.

Native Hawaiian religion is entwined in the environment. Many Native Hawaiians practice various forms of Christianity, due to the influence of missionaries, but others are returning to their indigenous religion, *Ho'omana*. One island, Kaho'olawe, has become a place for the reinvigoration of religion and environment. Kaho'olawe was initially a penal colony, and in 1864 it was transformed to ranch land (Hartwell 1996). The animals ate much of the vegetation and left a barren landscape. Later, Kaho'olawe became a U.S. Navy bombing practice ground, which decimated the landscape further and littered it with unexploded ordnance. This has left the island barren and the environment is severely damaged. Erosion is unchecked. In 1976 an organization called Protect Kaho'olawe 'Ohana formed, seeking to stop Navy bombing and to regain the island for Native Hawaiian spiritual observances.

Through protest and political action, 'Ohana first gained the right to have access to the island forty days per year, and then the Navy returned the island to the state in 1989, which will allow only traditional Hawaiian use (no commercial activity). Access to the island is only available by boat. The 'Ohana travel to the island when access is granted, bringing spiritual leaders, community members, and Native Hawaiians who wish to reconnect with their spirituality and identity. Kaho'olawe is an important island spiritually because it is the site of ceremonies honoring Lono, the god of fertility and agriculture. Makahiki, a four-month celebration, is now celebrated at Kaho'olawe annually. Instead of following tradition precisely, celebrants must modify the schedule, avoiding conflict with access rights, modern responsibilities, and the desolate state of the environment on the island—chants promoting growth on the island have been added to ceremonies.

Monies are allocated for the removal of the unexploded ordnance, but only small areas of the island are currently safe. To bring vegetation back to the island, Native Hawaiians are bringing in local vegetation from other islands, building catchments to retain rain water, and the Navy is blasting holes in the soil to plant drought-resistant trees. Native Hawaiians are also calling upon Lono to grant fertility and growth on the island. The people who visit Kaho'olawe regularly are seeing the results of their labor as the island becomes green and the vegetation begins to thrive.

Kalo is the plant that is used to make *poi*. It is a root crop, similar to potatoes. Some varieties of *kalo* are grown in irrigated terraces (the most common) and others are dry crops. *Poi* is a traditional Hawaiian food that was once a dominant part of the island diet. It is rich in vitamins and minerals, and is still produced today—often for tourists to sample or for celebratory feasts. *Kalo* is a demanding crop to farm, and the harvest and planting work is still done manually. A lack of water supply, EPA regulations, land shortages, and an expensive cost of living discourage farmers. Many of the *kalo* farmers are Japanese, but Hawaiian families are returning to this profession (see the story of Clarence Eli Kaona in Hartwell 1996). Kaona, after spending several years on the mainland, returned to the Hawaiian Islands to continue his father's kalo growing business upon his death. Hawaiians reclaiming a traditional profession is an example of the rediscovery of local roots and identity.

Prior to the arrival of missionaries, Hawaiian was a spoken language. Then the Calvinist missionaries began to develop a written language and a Hawaiian Bible (Hartwell 1996). King Kamehameha II began promoting the teaching of the written Hawaiian language. Literate Hawaiians authored chants, traditions, histories, and newspapers. In 1886, with the overthrow of Queen Lili'uokalani came the passing of a law prohibiting teaching of Hawaiian and making English the official language. With the passage of this law, the language was at risk of being lost. Today the Hawaiian language is being revived. Immersion programs at preschools began in the mid 1980's. In 1986, the use of Hawaiian language in schools was legalized by the state legislature (Hartwell 1996). This act revoked a 90-year-old law prohibiting the use of Hawaiian as a primary teaching language. Hawaiian language instruction is available at all levels: from preschool through college.

Examples of Hybridity

Expressions of hybridity exist among Native Hawaiians. For example, Native Hawaiians speak traditional Hawaiian, pidgin (a Hawaiian version of English), and English. The languages of the locals and the colonizers exist, alongside a third language that is the localized version of the colonizer's language. Native Hawaiians incorporate religions, practicing Christianity and maintaining elements of their pre-contact spirituality. Examples of hybridity also exist in the political realm, in the form of a Hawaiian political party, a Hawaiian constitution, a definition of naturalized subjects of Hawai'i, possession of national symbols (e.g. anthem, flag, and coat of arms). The Hawaiian political party and constitution are hybrids because they take the form of Western democratic political bodies but reflect Hawaiian values and norms. The definition of naturalized subjects mirrors the colonizer's form, with the exception that members are called subjects (Hawai'i was a monarchy) instead of citizens. The anthem, flag, and coat of arms are not indigenous in the form that they take, but the images and words that make up these symbols reflect the Hawaiian culture. In language, religion, and politics, the Native Hawaiians express hybrid identities.

Ho'oponopono is a Hawaiian form of forgiveness and conflict resolution. The word *ho'oponopono* "literally means "to make right, to correct." It refers to a Hawaiian form of conflict resolution and discussion that "opens" the "closed" relations between people which have been entangled by hurt feelings and consequent painful retaliations" (Ito 1999: 116). It has a long tradition in Native Hawaiian culture, and remains a part of the culture—with some new ways of performing the act. There are three ways that *ho'oponopono* is practiced: privately amongst friends and family, in the church, or in family therapy (Ito 1999). The institutionalization of this practice, in church or in therapy, shows how Native Hawaiians still value the local culture but are willing to allow it to take on elements of the colonial culture to create a new form of *ho'oponopono*. There are four parts of *ho'oponopono*: a prayer opens the process, then people open themselves up and discuss their problems, next these problems are "cut" out of the relationships, and finally the parties forgive each other and seal this forgiveness

Global, Local, and/or Hybrid Identities

with a feast (Ito 1999). The process is very similar in the three different settings, but it is less formal in the private settings. It is most common to find people using *ho'oponopono* privately amongst friends.

Medicine is another arena that is becoming hybridized. Hawaiian *lapa'au* (healing) is coming back into practice. Healers practice four different types of methods: *ho'oponopono* (discussed in the previous paragraphs), *kupuna la'au lapa'au* (healing with medicinal plants), *lomi* (massage), and *la'au kahea* (channeling God's healing power). Few elders passed Hawaiian healing techniques on to the younger generations. But the practitioners who remain gather regularly, exchanging expertise, advice for dealing with the medical establishment, or concerns about liability (Hartwell 1996). Communities of Native Hawaiian healers, such as Kupuna La'au Lapa'au o Hawai'i, are developing systems of credentialism in order to match the medical establishment more closely. Young people participate in the meetings of Native Hawaiian healers, learning from the elders and developing apprenticeship programs to continue the tradition. A hybrid medicine is emerging that contains elements of traditional Hawaiian healing and cosmopolitan medicine.

Native Hawaiian music (*mele*) is merging with other culture's music. One example is Jawaiian, a mixture of Jamaican and Hawaiian music, which includes elements of both types of music and yet it is an entirely new form of music (Hartwell 1996). In previous generations, Hawaiian musicians have added sounds from jazz, opera, rock or country-western style music. Native Hawaiian music is a hybrid expression of culture. In this music, Hawaiian instruments are common, but themes reveal the colonial experience (e.g. songs about the destruction of Hawaiian land or Caucasian plantation bosses) and the modernization of Native Hawaiians. Some songs are sung in Hawaiian and others in English. Some Native Hawaiian people entering the music business express their Hawaiian culture by seeking to avoid the "dog-eat-dog" competitiveness of the contemporary music business. Native Hawaiian music is hybrid in its sound, language, the instruments, themes of the lyrics, and sometimes in the way business is conducted.

INTERACTIONS WITH THE STATE

Within State boundaries there is "a conflict between old-style territorial nationalism and a new, ethnically driven interventionalism" (Giddens 2000:36). Increasing regional power is beneficial to indigenous Nations. Hybridity gives Native Hawaiians an edge in their interactions with the state of Hawai'i and with the United States federal government. Although these governing systems were initially foreign, the experience of living as internal colonies forced the Native Hawaiians to become familiar with the system. Given an understanding of the colonizer's government, Native Hawaiians can work with the system to bring change.

In the local arena, Native Hawaiians are defending against anti-affirmative action and reverse discrimination lawsuits. These suits are aimed at State of Hawai'i agencies that were created to protect the Native Hawaiians and their culture. The community engages in protests at the airport, refuses to renew licenses for cars and drivers, and organizes protest rallies. In the negotiations with the federal government, the Native Hawaiians are seeking to assert their independence from the United States, honoring previous agreements and reversing the unlawful occupation of the islands. The results of this work include an apology bill issued in 1993 (Public Law Number 103–150). The Native Hawaiian Nation publishes reports and opinion pieces on the invasion of Hawai'i, asserts their right to self-govern, and issues Hawaiian passports. Native Hawaiian sovereignty movement organizations are mobilizing against the State structure to create the space for change.

If efforts on the local level are unsuccessful, then Native Hawaiians can appeal to international governing organizations. To achieve this, Native Hawaiians are appealing to the United Nations for freedom from the United States government. On July 5, 2001 a complaint was filed with by the Hawaiian Kingdom with the United Nations Security Council on behalf of Native Hawaiians. The Hawaiian Kingdom asserts that Hawai'i has been unlawfully occupied by the United States since 1898, violating Hawaiian law, treaties between the United States and Hawai'i, and international law (specifically 1907 Hague Regulations). The Hawaiian Kingdom asks that an inquiry be conducted to investigate the merits of the complaint and recommend appropriate future actions. Native Hawaiians are active in international governing organizations, with a member of their movement on the board of the United Nations' Permanent Forum on Indigenous Issues. International governmental and non-governmental institutions offer a different platform for the airing of grievances about self-determination from colonial (internal or external) powers. Because of its years as an occupied territory and now an internal colony, Native Hawaiians are able to state their claims in multiple settings, using contextually relevant arguments in each situation.

Even with hybridity, the State maintains an advantage in the form of its monopoly on the use of force. States have used their power to create both diversity within the State and uniformity across State organizations—resulting in a schizophrenic cultural force (Wallerstein 1997a). By going to the State, Native Hawaiians reaffirm the relevance of the State. The process results in the integration of the movement "into the very system it is opposing . . . which however partially legitimates these structures" (Wallerstein 1997a: 100). This has been the case for Native Hawaiians, who shape their sovereignty claims to match the federal and international systems. While trying to recreate their own meaning for their identity, the Native Hawaiians working within the bounds created by outsiders are strengthening the State structure. Unless Native Hawaiians assert their rights, disregarding the State, they empower the State while protesting against it.

CONCLUSION

Indigenous Nations living as internal colonies must live according to the laws and norms of the external groups. In this setting, indigenous Nations labor to maintain the integrity of their own culture while learning to exist within the setting created by the outsiders. Out of this experience, hybrid identities emerge. Indigenous Nations have been living as hybrids since colonialism first began, as the colonizer's world developed around them. Given their distinctive national contexts, indigenous Nations relate to globalizing processes differently. Indigenous Nations are able to reach beyond the local as a result of their experience in the colonial and post-colonial eras. They experience cosmopolitanism distinctly when compared to immigrants and Diasporas. They are involuntary outsiders—the other world moved into their realm. Many indigenous Nations have been generating tools for dealing with outsiders since the time of European expansion.

Hybridity was initially an outcome of oppression, a way of negotiating stability for the fragile dual identity (DuBois 1996 [1903]; Gandhi 1998). The expansion of globalization brings hybridity to the privileged and the disadvantaged. Universalizing processes are acting simultaneously with localizing processes. A global culture is spreading, and as it comes in contact with various localities a hybrid identity develops. Hybridity is about creativity and cultural imagination (Lo 2002). Those who occupy hybrid spaces benefit from having an understanding of both local knowledge and global cosmopolitanism. The hybrid identity is a unique space.

The emergence of a hybrid identity, which includes elements of the global and local cultures, promotes agency. Instead of a homogenization, assimilation, or Westernization, the expression of a hybrid identity is agentic. Hybridity can create a common system of ethics (Gandhi 1998), which it also exemplifies. The free expression of culture is a human right. The expression of culture is a collective act performed by individuals. The individual makes up the whole, and expresses the identity of the whole. The embodiment of a hybrid identity is an act of freedom, and is to be protected under third generation human rights doctrine. Via hybridity, a reflexive definition of justice, morality, and ethics will form.

Chapter Six
New Applications of Human Rights

Legal scholars and philosophers examine human rights. Sociological study of human rights is uncommon (exceptions include Howard and Donnelly 1986; Mitchell, Howard, and Donnelly 1987; and Howard 1995). Human rights are a collective good, and as such it is the perfect subject of study for sociologists. A sociological study of human rights includes the study of the processes underlying the adoption of human rights principles. Analysis of the conception of human rights over time is another element of the sociological study of human rights. Sociologists from many epistemological backgrounds can make a contribution to the examination of human rights.

In this chapter I begin by asserting that the study of human rights is a topic for sociological analysis. This is followed by a definition of human rights, and a presentation of human rights doctrine regarding indigenous peoples. I define and identify three generations of human rights as expressed in doctrine and the protections they provide. Then I examine human rights empirically in two cases: the Native Hawaiian sovereignty movement and the Zapatistas movement. After looking at the protections available from the State structure, I look at the Universal Declaration of Human Rights. This allows me to see which body—either the State constitution or the international human rights doctrine—offers greater protections for the rights that indigenous Nations seek. I conclude with my findings and ideas for future research.

HUMAN RIGHTS

Human rights encompass the right to *"what is minimally necessary to live one's life as a human being"* (Howard 1995:14). Human rights protect human agency and by extension protect human agents (Ignatieff 2001). Ideas of what is minimally necessary to live, what protects agency, and what protects agents are socially constructed. Thus, the empirical expression of human rights is not static, but shifts as the socially defined meaning changes. In this context basic human rights generally consist of the right to subsistence; protections from cruel and unusual punishments; and the freedom *from* oppression, interference, or abuse. Rights to something (e.g. the right to life) are positive liberties and freedoms from something (e.g. freedom from degradation) are negative liberties.

The ways that human rights can be defined and operationalized are highly controversial. Human rights must be compatible with moral pluralism: not seeking to change cultures, but promoting the integration of human rights protections (Gutmann 2001). This is not to say that they must comply with every belief system, because sometimes belief systems can be the most discriminatory, committing human rights violations (Gutmann 2001). Human rights must coexist with the liberal State and moral pluralism. Although by moral philosophical thinking this should be easy to achieve, the empirical reality is sometimes rife with conflict.

Doctrine granting freedoms have gone through multiple iterations over the years. The goals of the doctrine fall into three generations of ideology. First generation human rights doctrine protects the rights of individuals from the State. These are negative rights and are framed in a manner that pits the individual against the State. Second generation human rights doctrine offers positive rights for individual members of groups. With third generation human rights, collective human rights are recognized.

The Proposed American Declaration of the Rights of Indigenous Peoples[1] (1997) illustrates all three generations of human rights. Rights provided for in this document include: the eradication of poverty and the right to development; protections of indigenous culture; the absence of discrimination; prohibition of militarization of indigenous lands; protection from forced assimilation; and the right to cultural development and integrity. The prohibition of militarization of indigenous lands and protection from forced assimilation are examples of first generation human rights. The absence of discrimination and the eradication of poverty are examples of second generation human rights. Here these protections are aimed at one group (indigenous peoples), but they are rights that will be enjoyed by individuals. The right to development, protections of indigenous culture, and the right to cultural development and integrity are examples of third generation human rights.

First Generation Human Rights

The installation of human rights treaties following World War II created a new protection for individuals. These rights are rooted in liberalism, and are negative rights—"freedoms from" acts that would hinder liberty. First generation human rights put the individual in opposition to the State. Under first generation human rights, the individual is protected from the State. First generation human rights can be exemplified by documents such as the Bill of Rights (see Appendix One) and the United States Constitution. For example, the Bill of Rights provides the individual with the freedom from laws that would hinder free speech (Amendment I), protects persons from unreasonable searches and seizures (Amendment IV), and protects the individual from punishment that is cruel and unusual (Amendment VIII).

Here I will present other examples of first generation human rights, many of which apply specifically to indigenous peoples. First generation human rights protect indigenous peoples from forced evictions (UN Draft Declaration on the Rights of Indigenous Peoples,[2] Part II, Article 10, 1994 as printed in Anaya 1996 and The International Labour Organization Convention Number 169,[3] Article 16.1 1989). A second example of individuals being protected from the power of the State is in the right of indigenous peoples "to have their legal personality fully recognized by the states within their systems" (Proposed American Declaration of the Rights of Indigenous Peoples, Article IV 1997 as printed in Anaya 1996:221). Indigenous peoples are also entitled to the right to "human rights and fundamental freedoms without hindrance or discrimination" (United Nations Conference on Environment and Development, Chapter 26, Section 26.1 1992 in Anaya 1996:204). Other human rights doctrine, grants indigenous peoples and Nations "the right to life, and to freedom from oppression, discrimination, and aggression" (Declaration of Principles on the Rights of Indigenous Peoples[4] 1987 in Anaya 1996:190). Indigenous peoples' rights are protected under another doctrine, which grants them the right "to use lands not exclusively occupied by them, but to which they have traditionally had access for their subsistence and traditional activities" (International Labour Organization Convention Number 169, Article 14.1 1989). This is a protection from the State in the event that indigenous peoples must cross federally owned lands in order to access their usual and accustomed places.

Second Generation Human Rights

Second generation human rights are rights for types of individuals, those who are members of a class of persons, not rights for collectives. They may offer protections to women, minorities, people with disabilities, or even the right to social security. This is the stage when moral equality enters into human rights doctrine. Second generation human rights are positive rights, such as the right to health care or social security. For example, second generation human rights provide for the right to an adequate standard of living for all people (United Nations Universal Declaration of Human Rights, Article 25 1948). Similarly, the United Nations Draft Declaration on the Rights of Indigenous Peoples (1994) protects the rights of indigenous peoples to developments of health, housing, economic, and social programs.

Third Generation Human Rights

Third generation rights, rights due to collectives, are emerging. Collective rights, such as the right to a cultural identity, can extend individual freedoms and liberty. UNICEF's document protecting cultural rights is an example of third generation human rights. Rights to ancestral lands, the rights to cultural protections, and language are inherently collective rights. An individual cannot practice the right to language, because this is something that is shared. Collective rights can be misconstrued as not pertaining to individuals, or even hindering individual freedoms. Yet, the denial of collective rights does inhibit freedoms. There are many examples of collective rights, including the protection of the rights of Nations (Convention on the Prevention of the Crime of Genocide and the International Covenant on Civil and Political Rights in Paxman 1989). Other examples of third generation rights include the right to nationality (United Nations Universal Declaration of Human Rights, Article 15 1948) and the freedom from arbitrary deprivation of nationality (United Nations Universal Declaration of Human Rights, Article 15 1948 and Convention on the Reduction of Statelessness, Article 9 1961 in Institutional Centre for Ethnic Studies and David Hawk 1995). Another example of collective rights includes the provision for the protection of cultural diversity "as a source of exchange, innovation and creativity, cultural diversity is as necessary for humankind as biodiversity is for nature" (Universal Draft Declaration on Cultural Diversity,[5] Article 1 2001).

There are many examples of third generation human rights pertaining specifically to indigenous peoples, such as the "right to maintain and develop their distinct identities and characteristics, including the right to identify themselves as indigenous and be recognized as such" (The United Nations Draft Declaration on the Rights of Indigenous Peoples, Part II, Article 8 1994 in Anaya 1996:210). In another example of third generation human rights, indigenous peoples have the right to "culture, religion, education, information, media, health, housing, employment, social welfare, economic activities, land and resources management, environment" (The United Nations Draft Declaration on the Rights of Indigenous Peoples: Part VII Article 31 1994 in Anaya 1996:214). Article Five of the International Labour Organization's Convention Number 169 (1989) provides similar rights. Further, indigenous peoples are entitled to "the right to the common ownership of their traditional land sufficient in terms of area and quality for the preservation and development of their particular ways of life" (Resolution on Action Required Internationally To Provide Effective Protection for Indigenous Peoples[6] 1994 in Anaya 1996:217).

The preamble of the Proposed American Declaration of the Rights of Indigenous Peoples (in Anaya 1996) recognizes the right to exercise collective freedoms that can be enjoyed by all individuals (also mentioned in section 2, Article 2, number 2 of this document). The Declaration of Principles on the Rights of Indigenous Peoples (1987 in Anaya 1996) provides the right of indigenous Nations and peoples to the control of their ancestral lands. Third generation human rights protections of indigenous peoples "include the right of these peoples to participate in the use, management and conservation of these resources" (International Labour Organization Convention Number 169, Article 15.1 1989).

Under other third generation human rights protections, indigenous peoples are entitled to the freedom to determine their political status and pursue the community's goals for economic, social, and cultural development (United Nations Draft Declaration on the Rights of Indigenous Peoples 1994). The right to self-determination, a third generation human right, is another freedom that is observed collectively. This right is protected in at least seven human rights documents: United Nations Declaration on the Granting of Independence to Colonial Countries and Peoples[7] (1960); United Nations International Covenant on Civil and Political Rights[8] (1976); Draft Declaration of Principles for the Defense of the Indigenous Nations and Peoples of the Western Hemisphere[9] (1977); Declaration of Principles on the Rights of Indigenous Peoples (1987); International Labour Organization Convention Number 169 (1989); United Nations Draft Declaration on the Rights of Indigenous Peoples (1994); and the Proposed American Declaration of the Rights of Indigenous Peoples (1997).

INDIGENOUS RIGHTS AS HUMAN RIGHTS

For indigenous Nations seeking rights and freedoms, the best solution may not be to adhere to an historical document or agreement (Kymlicka 1995; Trask, H. 1999). This would mean adherence to an agreement that may have been signed under duress or with a lack of understanding. It may not be possible to fully understand the circumstances surrounding the initial agreement, given competing histories. Many of the agreements are out of date, "patently unfair," or were signed under duress or in ignorance.

Indigenous Nations need another source of rights, freedoms, and protections beyond the States that they exist within as internal colonies. Rights granted by human rights treaties, allow for the maintenance of cultural integrity (Corntassel and Primeau 1995). The United Nations is interested in protecting indigenous peoples, forming a working group and drafting a Declaration of Indigenous rights, designed to "advance the intermediate indigenous goal of holding states accountable to international standards of respect and protection for indigenous peoples, lands, resources, and cultures" (Lam 1992:607–608). International human rights doctrine can be a protector of freedoms and rights. Indigenous Nations are pushing international human rights beyond the limits of State-centered structures. Now agents—instead of objects—of human rights, indigenous Nations are defining and attaining access to human rights (Anaya 1996).

Human rights can be a means of attaining the rights to self-determination, self-government, the maintenance and development of culture, and the right to hold land collectively. Indigenous Nations can seek human rights as a means to protect freedom and agency: "the great advantage of individual human rights is that they allow, even encourage, persons occupying dishonored categories to join together to collectively pressure for recognition of their human rights" (Howard 1995:160). Indigenous Nations exist outside the realm of many State governing bodies. As additional policies are adopted, for example the United Nations Declaration on the Rights of Indigenous Peoples and the UNICEF Declaration on Cultural Diversity, the definition of human rights is expanding.

The International Labor Organization has been concerned with indigenous and tribal peoples, adopting conventions in 1957 and 1989 (Symonides and Volodin 2001). Many pieces of human rights doctrine (e.g. Declaration of Principles on the Rights of Indigenous Peoples 1987; International Labour Organization Convention Number 169 1989; United Nations Draft Declaration on the Rights of Indigenous Peoples 1994; and Proposed American Declaration of the Rights of Indigenous Peoples 1997) explicitly state that indigenous peoples and Nations are entitled to human rights protections and freedoms. In 2002 a Permanent Forum on Indigenous Issues was formed by the United Nations. This panel consists of eight indigenous experts (chosen by the indigenous communities) and eight experts elected by the Economic and Social Council. The Forum was created on the recommendation of the Commission on Human Rights and will report to the Economic and Social Council. Indigenous peoples around the globe will gain freedoms as they are able to attain greater rights of self-government, self-determination, and possibly the return of aboriginal homelands.

The worldview of indigenous Nations incorporates cosmology and spirituality into political and economic life and promotes a collective reference point instead of using the individual as the basis for rights (Maiguashca 1994). The cultural distinctness of indigenous Nations appeals to the international community, and can be mobilized as a resource. Ceremonies, stories, and art are all assets that are unique to indigenous communities. Using culture as a resource that can be mobilized might call attention to the indigenous groups seeking human rights protections. In this case, indigenous identity is a "good" that can be employed to assist in the expanded definition and enforcement of human rights.

FREEDOMS SOUGHT

Groups can seek the rights of a group against its members, called internal restrictions, or the rights of a group against the larger society, called external protections (Kymlicka 1995: 35). Native Hawaiians and the Zapatistas are, in most cases, seeking external protections. Because the Native Hawaiian sovereignty movement consists of multiple organizations that seek different rights and freedoms, I consider the claims of one organization here, Ka Lāhui Hawai'i. I then present the protections sought by the Zapatistas, as they are written in the letters from the Lacandón Jungle (see General Command of the Zapatista National Liberation Army 2002 [1993]; General Command of the Zapatista National Liberation Army 2002 [1994]; General Command of the Zapatista National Liberation Army 2002 [1995]; and General Command of the Zapatista National Liberation Army 2002 [1996]).

Ka Lāhui Hawai'i have five stated goals to end the United States occupation (Trask, H. 1999). They seek the resolution of historic claims related to the overthrow, misuse to native trust lands, violation of human and civil rights, and federally held lands and resources. Second, Ka Lāhui Hawai'i seeks an end to U.S. policy not recognizing Native Hawaiian sovereignty—including an end to the wardship status. They also request the recognition of Ka Lāhui as a Hawaiian Nation including jurisdiction over national assets, lands and natural resources. The fourth goal is a United States commitment to decolonize Hawai'i via the United Nations process for non-self-governing territories. Finally, Ka Lāhui Hawai'i seeks the restoration of traditional lands, national resources, ocean, and energy resources to the Ka Lāhui National Land Trust. These are all freedoms from the United States government, and follow a logical procession of first making good on historical claims, recognizing Hawaiian sovereignty and its political leadership, decolonization, and finally the return of lands.

In writings from the Lacandón Jungle, the Zapatistas assert the right to alter the government, and they seek to do so by working within the political system. The Zapatistas, a Mayan organization, seek to overthrow the Mexican government in order to reinstate a democratic system that is approved by the people, calling for the participation of Mexican civil society to strengthen the cause. The Zapatistas are seeking protections from an external society, the Mexican government. In addition the Zapatistas assert eleven demands: housing, land, employment, food, education, independence, democracy, liberty, justice, and peace. These demands are not protections from an external body or rights to freedoms from oppression within the organization (the Zapatistas). Instead, these are basic needs, which the democratic State has a duty to provide. The Zapatistas argue that these necessities have been denied of the Indians.

The Native Hawaiians seek the removal of an occupying force, the United States. This is a third generation human right, which grants the protection of a collective, in this case from an outside body. Although Ka Lāhui Hawai'i does not explicitly seek the basic rights and freedoms such as the right to housing, land, food, or education, this is implicit in their final request for the return of lands and the natural resources. Thus, the Native Hawaiians are implicitly seeking second generation human rights. The freedom from rule by a State that does not reflect the goals and desires of the citizens is a first generation human right, the type which protects individuals from the State. Here, the Zapatistas are seeking protection from the State of Mexico for all Mexicans. The basic needs demanded by the Zapatistas are examples of one empirical assertion of what is minimally necessary to maintain human life, and are second generation human rights. Both the Native Hawaiians and the Zapatistas are appealing to the State government (the United States and Mexico, respectively) and to international governing bodies to attain the rights that they seek.

NATIVE HAWAIIANS AS AN EXAMPLE

For Native Hawaiians, there are two sources of rights and freedoms within the federal structure: the State of Hawai'i's constitution or the United States constitution. There is also an Indian Civil Rights Act (a federal law), which Native Hawaiians might employ to assert their rights.[10] The Akaka Bill is presently under consideration in the United States Congress, which would grant Native Hawaiians tribal status. Earlier a congressional resolution known as U.S. Public Law 103–150 (1993, see Appendix 2) was passed, "acknowledging and apologizing for historical wrongs against Native Hawaiians" (Anaya 1996:151–152). The State of Hawai'i and the United States recognize that Native Hawaiians have been wronged and deserve special considerations.

The State of Hawai'i's constitution might provide rights to Native Hawaiians. In this document, the Hawaiian Homes Commission Act is re-established, including the state's acceptance of Act and the responsibilities it entails (The Constitution of the State of Hawai'i, Article XII, Section 2, see Appendix Three). The Hawaiian Homes Commission Act establishes the Office of Hawaiian Affairs, which has a nine member board of trustees who manage trust lands and proceeds. The State of Hawai'i's constitution provides for the management of Hawaiian lands and funds. In addition to this support, "the State reaffirms and shall protect all rights, customarily and traditionally exercised for subsistence, cultural and religious purposes" (The Constitution of the State of Hawai'i, Article XII, Section 7, see Appendix Three). This act illustrates that the state recognizes the importance of the continuance of the Native Hawaiian culture and peoples.

The United States Constitution is cited as the source of rights and freedoms for Americans. Applying it to the case of the Native Hawaiians,[11] Americans by conquest, it offers little that would further the goals of Ka Lāhui Hawai'i. The United States Constitution grants rights to American citizens, presuming that their allegiance is first to the Federal Government and that the rights they seek can be granted and protected by this body. The desire for greater freedom from rule by the United States cannot be sought under any protections provided by the Constitution. Native Hawaiians exist outside of the realm of the Constitution, which is an imposed structure (Trask, H. 1999). Seeking rights or protections under the United States government would risk reaffirming the Native Hawaiians' status as an internal colony and a Nation without a State.

Citizenship might seem like a feasible way to transcend difference and inequality, for Native Hawaiians to attain rights as individuals if not as a community. Yet in participatory democracies, disadvantaged groups are often silenced (Gutmann 1980, Young 1998). Aristotle foretold this problem, referring to democracy as the tyranny of the masses. Instead of presenting an opportunity, existing oppression is reproduced (Young 1998). Native Hawaiians do not make up a majority population in Hawai'i or the United States, and are economically and politically disadvantaged.

Changing the face of citizenship might provide opportunities to Native Hawaiians. Group representation might be an answer to the Native Hawaiian call for increased rights of self-government. Under a system of group representation, fairness is institutionalized and decisions can take into account local knowledge (Young 1998). Special rights to protect language and culture would also be provided to promote social justice (Young 1998). Citizenship in this format would provide both universal and special rights, allowing greater freedoms to all citizens while acknowledging their different needs. With this shift in citizenship, Native Hawaiians would attain protections that are not available under the United States Constitution as it stands.

The United States has also enacted the Indian Civil Rights act (passed in 1968, see Appendix Four), designed to protect individual American Indians. Native Hawaiians do not have a tribal structure that is recognized by the federal government, and so the application of this law to their case is unclear. In accordance with this act, American Indians are protected from any tribal government laws that would violate the named civil rights. These rights include: freedom of speech and religion; freedom from unreasonable search and seizures; freedom from prosecution more than once for a single offence; cannot be compelled to testify against self in a criminal case; private property cannot be taken without compensation; right to a speedy trial, to be informed of charges, confront witnesses, subpoena witnesses, to be assisted by a lawyer (at the individual's expense); freedom from excessive bail, cruel and unusual punishment; equal protection of the laws and freedom from deprivation of liberty or property without due process of the law; freedom from any bill of attainder or ex post facto law; the right to a trial by jury of no less than six persons (Indian Civil Rights Act 1968). These are first generation human rights designed to protect the freedoms of individual members of the tribe from the tribal government.

The Indian Civil Rights Act is designed to protect individual tribal members from the power of the tribal government, much like the Bill of Rights protects citizens of the United States from its government. In the case of the Native Hawaiians, there is no tribal government. Even the Office of Hawaiian Affairs cannot be called a tribal government, as it is a Hawaiian State agency. The freedoms that the Native Hawaiians seek from the United States are not from a tribal governing body. For this reason, the Indian Civil Rights Act is irrelevant to Native Hawaiians, even if it applies to them under federal doctrine. The law protects them from an entity that does not exist, and protects rights that do not pertain to the goals of the Native Hawaiians.

THE ZAPATISTAS AS AN EXAMPLE

The Mexican constitution presents little opportunity for expanded rights to indigenous peoples. The constitution protects every person in the United

Mexican States. Yet citizenship is limited to those who have an honest means of livelihood. Without citizenship, Mexicans cannot: vote, be elected to office, gather to discuss political affairs, bear arms in defense of the Republic, or exercise the right of petition (Constitution of Mexico). There are no special rights for indigenous peoples in the Constitution of Mexico.

The Law of Rights and Indigenous Culture,[12] passed in April 2001, creates an opportunity for indigenous peoples within the State of Mexico to attain greater rights and freedoms. The Law of Rights and Indigenous Culture offers an array of rights to indigenous peoples: to develop and practice traditional medicine, access to health care, the right to education in indigenous languages, rights and equality of women, prohibition of displacement and expulsion, the right to return to lands that people were expelled from, autonomy of indigenous towns, to institute traditional systems of justice, provisions for translators in State agencies and courts, protection and development of indigenous culture, and labor protections (for adults and minors). In addition to this, the State will act as a mediator between indigenous groups and private companies or adjacent landholders. The State also offers to assist in creating budgets and development plans.

The Law of Rights and Indigenous Culture was written with the consultation of the Zapatistas. Although Fox initially negotiated with the Zapatistas in the writing of the bill, the alterations made by the federal congress and approved by the State legislatures left the document unsatisfactory to the Zapatistas. This version that passed the legislature was a watered down version of what they had previously negotiated. In an advertisement that the Zapatistas published in newspapers, they warned that the Bill would divide the Nation and weaken indigenous peoples ("Mexico OKs Indian Rights Bill" 2001). The failing of this document is its inability to recognize the historic roots of the demands of indigenous peoples and the need to acknowledge indigenous peoples as a collective body (Agustin and Cortéz 2001). Under this document, the power is still in the hands of the State.

PROTECTIONS UNDER THE UNIVERSAL DECLARATION OF HUMAN RIGHTS

The Universal Declaration of Human Rights consists of a preamble and thirty articles which grant rights to all people. These rights are due to all people. Articles 15, 17, and 21 (see Appendix Five) are examples of rights due to the Hawaiians, which have been violated by the United States (Trask, H. 1999). Article 15 assures that there shall be no arbitrary deprivation of nationality. The last Queen of Hawai'i gave up her rule to the United States under duress. That act was not representative of the

Hawaiian people giving up their nationality. Thus, it seems fair to charge that Hawaiians have been arbitrarily denied their nationality. Article 17 protects people from the arbitrary deprivation of property. When Hawaiʻi became a United States Territory, land changed hands but this was without regard to the Hawaiians. Large portions of the lands that were supposed to be set aside for Hawaiian Homelands were leased out. The Hawaiian Homelands acreage makes up only a small portion of the islands, and less than one quarter of these lands have been distributed to Hawaiians. The majority of Hawaiians have experienced the arbitrary denial of property by the State of Hawaiʻi under the current system of allocating Hawaiian Homelands. Article 21 assures that the will of the people will be the basis of the authority of the government. The denial of self-determination of the Hawaiian people violates this provision.

The Zapatistas have also been denied the rights provided for in Articles 15 and 21 (see Appendix Five), as they claim that there was an unlawful taking of sovereignty and nationhood. Although many of the early writings (first through fourth declarations from the Lacandón Jungle) implicitly suggest that the Zapatistas wish to remain Mexicans, they strongly assert that the Mexican government does not represent Mexican people. The taking of nationhood is different in this case, but the fact remains that Mexicans feel that their identity has been hijacked by outsiders who do not represent their values and do not reflect the characteristics that they wish to be associated with the label Mexican. The claim is that the PRI government is denying the sovereignty of the Zapatistas, and the Mexican people. Again, the protections offered by the human rights doctrine would shelter the Zapatistas and the Mexicans, returning their sovereignty and their national identity.

The protections provided by Article 18 have also been violated in the experience of the Zapatistas. Following Chiapas' move to join Mexico in 1824, indigenous landowners were displaced by elites (Hayden 2002). Beginning in the 1940's, a land reform movement, known as the *ejido* system, was instituted in Mexico. This movement, designed to establish communally owned lands, was not embraced in Chiapas (Hayden 2002). Finally, a more overt form of deprivation of property began in 1970 and spans twenty years: 50,000 Indians were expelled from their communities (Hayden 2002). The rights of the indigenous peoples to be protected from the deprivation of property have been violated, via local elites, a land reform movement, and government policies.

Returning to the case of the Native Hawaiians, it is also possible to argue that Articles 18 of the human rights doctrine has been violated. In this case, it is the State of Hawaiʻi that is violating the Articles, but the United States, by not suing on behalf of the Hawaiians, is an accomplice.

Article 18 grants the right to freedom of religion. The case of Hawaiians being forced to break the law (initially) to gain access to Kahoʻolawe is one example of the limitations that the United States government has placed on religious practice by Hawaiians by taking land and allocating it without regard to the Hawaiian people. The Zapatistas do not explicitly ask for the freedom of religion in their statements. This is not one of the eleven items that they demand, but it might be implicitly included under the grounds that the freedom of religion is a form of liberty and independence. It is also possible that the influence of liberation theology and the promotion of Indigenous Catholicism, beginning in the late 1960's, satisfied the religious needs of the Zapatista community. Thus, it is not clear if the Zapatistas' rights due to them under Article 18 have been violated.

Article 25 grants the right to an adequate standard of living (including food, clothing, housing, medical care, social services, security in the event of unemployment, lack of livelihood in circumstances beyond the individual's control), which has also been hampered by the lack of distribution of Hawaiian Homelands properties. People evicted from lands to be developed have often been left living on the beaches or in cars. Their applications to the office allocating Hawaiian Homelands properties might be on file for years before action is taken, and meanwhile the families are not experiencing an adequate standard of living. These arguments might be more tenuous, but claims could be made on behalf of at least some Hawaiians (if not the community at large) that their rights under these two articles have been denied.

The Zapatistas are also seeking the right to an adequate standard of living. Among the list of eleven items that they are demanding from the Mexican government, the first five are directly related to establishing an adequate standard of living: housing, land, employment, food, and education. The expelling of roughly 50,000 Indians from their communities over the course of the 1970s to the early 1990's has left many indigenous Mexicans with no hope of land ownership. The landless *campesinos* of Chiapas have little hope of an adequate standard of living without outside intervention, either from the Mexican government or from the international community. The circumstance that the Zapatistas live in is clearly a violation of Article 25, the right to an adequate standard of living.

FINDINGS

The Native Hawaiians have been unable to overthrow the occupying force of the United States. Even as citizens of the United States, Native Hawaiians may not be entitled to assert their nationality, achieve self-determination, have their basic needs met, or receive compensation for their land (either via payment or repatriation of the land). As United States citizens they are entitled to the freedom to practice their religion, but this right has already been violated in spite of this protection. The Native Hawaiians have been denied the land and its resources, lack freedom of religion, and an adequate standard of living. These are a handful of human rights violations (second and third generation human rights) that the State of Hawai'i and the United States allow to persist. The protests of the Native Hawaiians have fallen upon deaf ears.

The freedoms sought by the Zapatistas remain unmet as we approach the fifth anniversary of the signing of the Indian Rights Bill. The Indian Rights Bill recently ratified by the Mexican congress might grant the Zapatistas another avenue for attaining the rights they seek: housing, land, employment, food, education, independence, democracy, liberty, justice, and peace. The Zapatistas heavily criticized the bill, calling it a watered-down version of the agreement that they negotiated in 1996 ("Mexico OKs Indian Rights Bill" 2001). Yet this bill may provide them with the legal platform to attain their demands by working within the Mexican political system.

The Zapatistas are governed by a State that they feel does not represent the Mexican citizens. They lack a basic standard of living: education, food, employment, land, housing, and employment. These are due to the Zapatistas under the Universal Declaration of human rights (all second generation human rights). The Zapatistas also lack a handful of third generation human rights: liberty, justice, and peace. As the fifth anniversary of the Indigenous Rights Bill approaches, the State of Mexico remains unable to stop the violations of these human rights.

Native Hawaiians the Zapatistas have been denied Human Rights that are due to them under the Universal Declaration of Human Rights. Native Hawaiians and the Zapatistas also fall under protections offered by at least a dozen international human rights declarations, including the Universal Draft Declaration on Cultural Diversity, the International Labor Organization Convention Number 169, and the United Nations Draft Declaration on the Rights of Indigenous Peoples. Both the Native Hawaiians and the Zapatistas have the right to appeal to the United Nations for further protections from human rights violations.

CONCLUSION

State documents granting rights and freedoms to citizens rarely recognize special rights to indigenous Nations. The State is foreign, made up of institutions and norms that reflect the settler society and not the indigenous one. Citizenship and the United States Constitution have failed to protect the Native Hawaiians rights to land ownership or access, self-determination, and self-government. The Zapatistas have failed to have their rights and freedoms protected by the Mexican Constitution and the Indigenous Bill of Rights. Human rights doctrine can offer freedoms and protections to indigenous Nations that States cannot. Under human rights doctrine, all individuals have equal moral worth and the right to a minimal standard of living. Indigenous Nations' claims for right to land, self-government, and self-determination are protected under the Universal Declaration of Human Rights and many other documents adopted by international governing organizations. Stopping the violation of human rights will end the limits on individual agency and provide greater freedom for individual members of indigenous Nations.

History has witnessed the shift in governing bodies from the city-state to the State, and now we may be on the cusp of a transition from the State to a global polity. Human and societal interdependencies are growing exponentially with globalization. Every member of the global society has a stake in another member's human rights. In an interdependent, transnational society, the obligation for upholding human rights for ourselves and others is in each person's hands.

Chapter Seven
Conclusion

Communication networks move images, words, and money around the world at the speed of light. Political bodies are globalizing, with the increasing role of regional and international governing bodies. Commodities are traded worldwide and people are moving more than ever as immigrants, travelers, refugees, students, or short term employees. Borders are becoming more fluid to allow the passing of goods, people, and communiqués. As globalization is spreading, "the major trajectory of globalization, however, is still from the center to the periphery" (Benhabib 2002). While it may seem that the processes of globalization are unpredictable, there is a direction of activity that benefits the core while the periphery suffers oppression. With this concluding chapter I will briefly summarize what the project has done, present findings, illustrate the contribution of this project to the literatures, and suggest ideas for future research.

DESCRIPTION OF THE PROJECT

Despite the absence of colonial structures in the classical form, indigenous peoples continue to suffer impediments to their freedom to live as distinct groups in their original homelands (Anaya 1996). Indigenous peoples are forced to submit to alien laws and institutions imposed upon them in their own homeland (Bennett 1978). They are internal colonies. This project looks at the experience of indigenous Nations to show how they are able to express their culture and citizenship to varying degrees within the given contexts. I explore one central research question: what are opportunities for indigenous groups to attain greater rights?

In Chapter Two, "Research Design," I discussed the theoretical goals of this paper and the methodology. With chapter Three, "On Indigenousness," I considered the definition of this concept, problematized indigenousness, described it as a relational concept, and concluded by considering "indigenous" as a means of legitimating communities. Chapter Four, "The Hawaiians," provided background information on the condition of Hawaiians at the time of contact, as a United States territory, and thru the Hawaiian Renaissance to the present day. In chapter five, "Global, Local, and/or Hybrid Identities," I defined global, local, and hybrid identity types and presented examples from the Native Hawaiian case. With chapter six, "New Applications of Human Rights," I identified three types of human rights doctrine: first, second, and third generation human rights. Using the case of the Native Hawaiians and the Mayans as examples, I compared the freedoms provided in State constitutions with those in international human rights doctrine.

FINDINGS

Indigenous groups live under legal rules and cultural norms of the external society most of the time. I began this project asking what are opportunities for indigenous groups to attain greater rights? Hybridity, human rights, and the relational concept illustrate the broadening of opportunity for indigenous Nations. As collectives and as individuals, indigenous peoples in the age of transition are in a position to reshape their identity and the global governance system.

Hybridity was initially an outcome of oppression, a way of negotiating stability for the fragile dual identity (DuBois 1996 [1903]; Gandhi 1998). Instead of a homogenization, assimilation, or Westernization, the expression of a hybrid identity is agentic. Those who occupy hybrid spaces benefit from having an understanding of both local knowledge and global cosmopolitanism. The expansion of globalization brings hybridity to the privileged. Prior to globalization, elites created the rules of the game and others were forced to conform, but globalization is shifting power structures. Indigenous peoples expressed hybrid identities early, and for this reason they are uniquely equipped to confront the pluralism of the globalizing world. They have the tools and experience needed to thrive. Opportunities for indigenous peoples are increased by hybridity which: gives indigenous peoples the ability to communicate across boundaries; allows indigenous peoples to reshape their identities in an agentic manner; and can produce a global structure that respects and offers space for indigenous Nations.

Native Hawaiians and the Mayans have been denied Human Rights that are due to them under the Universal Declaration of Human Rights. Native Hawaiians have appealed to the State of Hawai'i and to the United States government for over a century. The protests of the Native Hawaiians have fallen upon deaf ears. The Zapatistas have called for an overthrow of what they call a dictatorship and negotiated a bill of rights for the indigenous people. The Indian Rights Bill was then altered by the Mexican congress, without the approval of the Zapatistas. The claims of the Zapatistas remain unmet as we approach the fifth anniversary of the signing of the Indian Rights Bill. The Native Hawaiians (using Ka Lāhui Hawai'i as an example) have five stated goals: the resolution of historic claims related to lands, human and civil rights; an end to U.S. policy not recognizing Native Hawaiian sovereignty; the recognition of Ka Lāhui as a Hawaiian Nation; a United States commitment to decolonize Hawai'i; and the restoration of traditional lands, national resources, ocean and energy resources. They have achieved none of these goals. The Zapatistas seek to overthrow the Mexican government in order to reinstate a democratic system and demand: housing, land, employment, food, education, independence, democracy, liberty, justice, and peace. None of these claims have been achieved.

The failure Native Hawaiians and the Mayans might be explained by their ineffective strategies. Yet, it is also important to recognize the contextual factors that may influence the outcome. Both the United States and Mexico are democratic States, which are designed to be guided by the will of the peoples. Neither State is effectively meeting the basic needs of the Native Hawaiians or the Mayans. The State bodies do not reflect the values or the priorities of either group. Both the Native Hawaiians and the Zapatistas must appeal to the United Nations for further protections from human rights violations and expanded freedoms.

Native Hawaiians and the Mayans fall under protections offered by the United Nations in the Declaration of the Rights of Indigenous Peoples, the UNESCO Declaration on Cultural Diversity, and in the Universal Declaration of Human Rights. These are three of the handful of organizations and doctrine that protect the rights of indigenous peoples. Even as citizens of the United States, Native Hawaiians may not be entitled to assert their nationality, achieve self-determination, or to be compensated for their land (either via payment or repatriation of the land). The Indian Rights Bill recently ratified by the Mexican congress might grant the Zapatistas another avenue for attaining the rights they seek: housing, land, employment, food, education, independence, democracy, liberty, justice, and peace. This bill may provide them with the legal platform to attain their demands by working within the Mexican political system, but if it does not, the Declaration of Human Rights can protect the freedoms that the Zapatistas seek. Human rights doctrine can offer freedoms and protections to indigenous Nations that States cannot. These doctrine provide protections of indigenous persons' rights from the State (first generation human

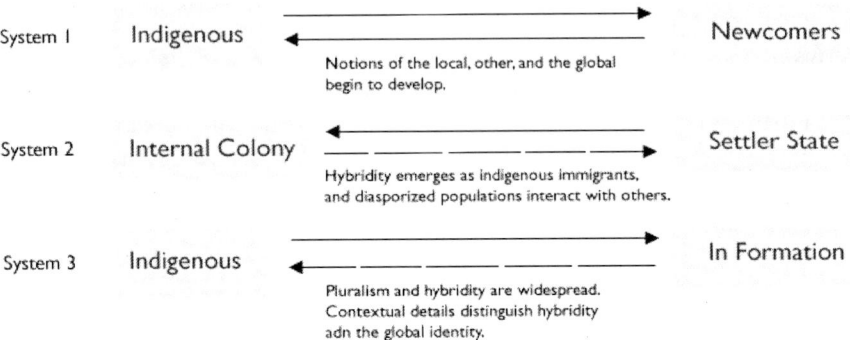

Figure 7.1 The Relational Concept and Identity

rights), they protect the rights of indigenous peoples as a class of individuals (second generation human rights), and they provide collective rights and freedoms (third generation human rights).

The relational concept is a useful tool for considering hybridity (see Figure 7.1). In System One, notions of the local, other, and the global are beginning to develop. This occurs during the early years of colonialism, global exploration and trade. As contact with outsiders grows, communities begin to develop a different understanding of what it means to be an insider and an outsider. In System Two, Hybridity emerges amongst indigenous peoples, immigrants, and diasporized populations. These groups are outsiders integrating elements of their "mother culture" with the culture of the settler State. In System Three pluralism and hybridity are widespread. Technologies, communication and travel are driving a standardization of the world population and the development of a global culture. At this point, the difference between the hybrid identity and the global identity is subtle: only local contextual details can distinguish the two. Applying the relational concept to human rights is illustrative (see Figure 7.2). In System One, there is no international human rights doctrine. In some States, constitutions that protect the rights of individuals are emerging. In System Two, the settler State has established first generation human rights. Second generation human rights are also in development, first within States and then in international governing organizations. Internal colonies have minimal input on the authoring of doctrine and the enforcement of human rights protections. In System Three, third generation rights are developing. Indigenous groups and others who were outsiders in System Two (e.g. developing States, regional groups, ethnic groups) are influential in the authoring of third generation human rights doctrine. The core *and*

Conclusion

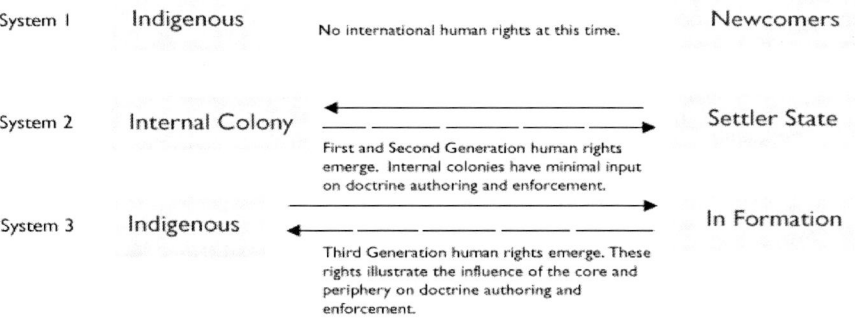

Figure 7.2 The Relational Concept and Human Rights

periphery contribute to the creation of third generation human rights and the enforcement of these protections.

Hybridity and human rights are two means for the attainment of greater rights for indigenous Nations. Hybridity provides a way to revision identity for indigenous Nations. With the hybrid identity, Nations can maintain cultural and legal independence and integrity. By incorporating elements of the global society, the Nations protect themselves from their downfall due to isolationism. The local and the global merging to create a hybrid identity is an asset to indigenous Nations and other oppressed populations. Human rights doctrine, which initially protected individuals from the State in the first generation and classes of people in the second generation, now provides collective rights. In claims for protections and freedoms made to the State, indigenous Nations threaten the State and simultaneously reinforce the relevance of the State. Human rights, however, offer indigenous Nations a unique opportunity to seek rights and freedoms. Organizations that promote human rights do so in the interest of broadening the importance of ethics and values. Their interest in the outcome of claims for human rights is not clouded by a risk of becoming illegitimate. The ability to seek rights from a political body that does not have a conflict of interest in the outcome allows indigenous Nations to be on equal ground with the State.

CONTRIBUTION TO KNOWLEDGE

My research stretches the boundaries of sociology, analyzing human rights. Applying sociological concepts to the study of human rights can aid in understanding its construction and operationalization. This project also brings new ideas to sociology by introducing territory. Studies of political movements and communities often take space and territory for granted. For indigenous Nations, territory is the vehicle of mobilization, often the object of contention. Finally, my research is an addition to the literature on world-systems theory: describing one example of how an anti-systemic movement can create new opportunities for self-determination—one that is not on the terms of the capitalist world-system, but instead created outside of that sphere.

The study of human rights is common in international studies, law, and policy research. Recently social scientists have begun to examine human rights (Howard and Donnelly 1986; Mitchell, Howard, and Donnelly 1987; and Howard 1995). This paper considers questions about how human rights are defined and how communities are challenging the current definitions. The claims of indigenous Nations are stretching the boundaries of the enforcement of human rights, asking for them to apply to groups. The application of human rights to collectives is a shift in how human rights are defined, understood, and applied. In the end individuals will still be the ones to exercise the human rights, as they are the ones who are members of collective organizations (here Nations). Indigenous groups are also asking for human rights as a matter of justice and morality.

This project considers how the conceptualization of human rights evolves over time, looking to the application of human rights to the indigenous case. This is one small, precise contribution to the study of the conceptualization of human rights. The most basic rights should presumably be the minimum of what a person needs to ensure the protection and preservation of his or her agency. Human rights is a social construct, which will further the sociological understanding of what society deems as being essential to the protection of humanity, and where humanity begins.

Political sociology has taken a narrow view of what it studies, with classical paradigms including only community and class. Territory and community interact to create a sense of place that is important to many groups, cultures, and individuals. This can become politicized when there are disputes over power to govern the territory. Territorial boundaries establish the boundaries of State sovereignty, it is "the engine of sovereignty" (Cooper n.d.). Although recent years have seen accelerated technological development that is less closely linked to land, communities continue to feel a tie to land. Territory, being the base of power and the container for the State, has a political role. The fact that indigenous Nations have to fight *so* hard against the State is indicative of the value of territory to States.

With this project I introduce the importance of territory to indigenous peoples, not because of its use value, but due to cultural ties and the relationship between the community and the land. For the State, the power container (Giddens 2000), territory determines the range of its might. It is also an economic resource to be exploited. To indigenous Nations, territory has a different meaning, and I work to make that explicit here. In defining indigenous, I include their unique tie to the land as one of the elements. In talking about the case of the Native Hawaiians, I discuss the relationship to the land and the history of the disputes that have taken place over rights of landholding and access. The inclusion of territory in future political sociological research is essential, and this project is a small start to further sociological study of territory, rights, freedoms and community.

Anti-systemic movements are working within the State and international system while attempting to shape an alternate framework for attaining political power within the State and internationally (Wallerstein 2000). Indigenous movements are among the many anti-systemic movements active today. Indigenous Nations can carve space for themselves in the midst of the capitalist world-system, although it is dominated by a culture that protects and perpetuates the free-market economy. For indigenous Nations, the collective is often more important than the individual. Maximizing economic gains is not the most important goal. The world-system is in an age of transition. When the new system emerges, the shape it takes may reveal the influence of indigenous culture, values, and norms. The bigness of the world-system does not prevent it from being influenced by shifts and change.

IN CONCLUSION

Indigenous Nations have options. The diversity and specificity of indigenous claims can be an advantage in creating solutions. This research produces a clearer picture of the indigenous experience in the globalizing world, and informs the literatures on globalization, political sociology, world-systems theory, and human rights. Below I present a handful of ideas for future research on human rights, territory, indigenous peoples, and hybridity. These suggestions are inspired by questions asked about this project and tangential ideas that crossed my mind in random moments.

The study of human rights in sociology is essential, as this is one way that groups are negotiating to create and maintain State and international norms of behavior. Human rights doctrine is a part of global governance, and understanding this concept will improve the sociological understanding of the structure and shape of international governing bodies. The welfare State, which has been declining in recent years, might be replaced by a more aggressive international human rights regime. First, second, and third generation human rights would likely be included in the doctrine that establishes this regime. It will be essential to continue further studies of the international governing bodies, but also of the State, which may change in response to the new protections that international governing bodies enforce. Further study might consider the first, second, and third generations of human rights in greater detail. An increasing number of documents could also be added to the list examined here, to further the understanding of collective rights and the right to sovereignty as human rights.

Additional comparisons of rights due to indigenous peoples under State constitutions and the United Nations Human Rights Doctrine are necessary. The democratic State is supposed to be an expression of the will of the people. As this project shows, in the case of the Native Hawaiians, the democratic State sometimes fails in this mission. Comparative studies of other internal colonies and the protections that the State provides will reveal a range of freedoms and protections that the State provides. At the same time, it is important to continue to refer back to the protections that international law provides. The evolution of international law is constant. Combing through additional international legal documents for rights and protections of indigenous Nations will reveal other bodies that are concerned with the welfare of internal colonies. This research will yield a better understanding of the different rights available to indigenous Nations, and possibly other oppressed groups, at the State and international levels. The results might expose a specific critique of liberal democracy and suggest new solutions to enact.

With the inclusion of territory, sociology expands its understanding of community. Many indigenous Nations view the land as a family member, as an ancestor, or as a link to the spiritual world. Within these cultures, land and its bounty are a part of the community. Land is not an inanimate object with a use value determined by location, natural resources below the surface, proximity to water and transportation, or fertility. The study of territory can broaden the relevance and application of sociological theory, compared to the exploitation of land and its resources. Although the market economy is widespread and has strong influence, exposure to foreign cultures is also increasing. It is necessary to understand other value systems, as the lives of individuals become interlinked in the global village. The health of the global village, which is constantly discovering new cultures and communities, relies upon increasing sociological understanding.

This project opens the door to future research in the study of indigenous peoples. The concept of indigenous can be valuable in sociological study. Additional case studies of groups that call themselves indigenous Nations would test and possibly verify the utility of the definition that I apply to the Native Hawaiians in this paper. It may also expose holes or errors that require adjustment. The perspective of a sociologist is distinct in that it focuses on interactions between individuals and groups and examines rules for living together. A sociological definition of this concept can make a unique contribution to studies of culture, law, and anthropology. Small samples could be gathered, selecting indigenous groups with similar colonial experiences from various regions, or comparing indigenous groups within the same region with varied colonial experiences. As an increasing number of cases are studied, a population of indigenous Nations will reveal itself, and can be studied in greater depth.

A deeper study of hybridity would be a contribution to sociological studies of identity, culture, and ethnicity. Doing further research on cultural expression within the Native Hawaiian community might yield a better understanding of the relationship between global, local, and hybrid. This might show patterns of individual or group expressions of identity. An in-depth study of the Native Hawaiian community with field research, extensive interviewing and surveys of participants and non-participants would allow me to flesh out the expression of identity in the Native Hawaiian community. A content analysis of Native Hawaiian literature, newspaper articles, or online articles would also be useful in establishing patterns of expression of identity. Further study of hybridity would also benefit from analysis of more cases, including indigenous and non-indigenous groups. Additional case studies with extensive data would allow for the discovery of trends in expressions of identity. It might become possible to identify particular settings or situations that would increase the likelihood that an individual or group would express a local, global, or hybrid identity.

Appendix One
Constitutional Amendments 1–10: The Bill of Rights[1]

Amendment I

Congress shall make no law respecting an establishment of religion, or prohibiting the free exercise thereof; or abridging the freedom of speech, or of the press; or the right of the people peaceably to assemble, and to petition the Government for a redress of grievances.

Amendment II

A well regulated Militia, being necessary to the security of a free State, the right of the people to keep and bear Arms, shall not be infringed.

Amendment III

No Soldier shall, in time of peace be quartered in any house, without the consent of the Owner, nor in time of war, but in a manner to be prescribed by law.

Amendment IV

The right of the people to be secure in their persons, houses, papers, and effects, against unreasonable searches and seizures, shall not be violated, and no Warrants shall issue, but upon probable cause, supported by Oath or affirmation, and particularly describing the place to be searched, and the persons or things to be seized.

Amendment V

No person shall be held to answer for a capital, or otherwise infamous crime, unless on a presentment or indictment of a Grand Jury, except in cases arising in the land or naval forces, or in the Militia, when in actual service in time of War or public danger; nor shall any person be subject for the same offence to be twice put in jeopardy of life or limb; nor shall be compelled in any criminal case to be a witness against himself, nor be deprived of life, liberty, or property, without due process of law; nor shall private property be taken for public use, without just compensation.

Amendment VI

In all criminal prosecutions, the accused shall enjoy the right to a speedy and public trial, by an impartial jury of the State and district wherein the crime shall have been committed, which district shall have been previously ascertained by law, and to be informed of the nature and cause of the accusation; to be confronted with the witnesses against him; to have compulsory process for obtaining witnesses in his favor, and to have the Assistance of Counsel for his defense.

Amendment VII

In suits at common law, where the value in controversy shall exceed twenty dollars, the right of trial by jury shall be preserved, and no fact tried by a jury, shall be otherwise reexamined in any Court of the United States, than according to the rules of the common law.

Amendment VIII

Excessive bail shall not be required, nor excessive fines imposed, nor cruel and unusual punishments inflicted.

Amendment IX

The enumeration in the Constitution, of certain rights, shall not be construed to deny or disparage others retained by the people.

Amendment X

The powers not delegated to the United States by the Constitution, nor prohibited by it to the States, are reserved to the States respectively, or to the people.

Appendix Two
United States Public Law 103–150[1]

To acknowledge the 100th anniversary of the January 17, 1893 overthrow of the Kingdom of Hawaii, and to offer an apology to Native Hawaiians on behalf of the United States for the overthrow of the Kingdom of Hawaii.

Whereas, prior to the arrival of the first Europeans in 1778, the Native Hawaiian people lived in a highly organized, self-sufficient, subsistent social system based on communal land tenure with a sophisticated language, culture, and religion;

Whereas, a unified monarchical government of the Hawaiian Islands was established in 1810 under Kamehameha I, the first King of Hawaii;

Whereas, from 1826 until 1893, the United States recognized the independence of the Kingdom of Hawaii, extended full and complete diplomatic recognition to the Hawaiian Government, and entered into treaties and conventions with the Hawaiian monarchs to govern commerce and navigation in 1826, 1842, 1849, 1875, and 1887;

Whereas, the Congregational Church (now known as the United Church of Christ), through its American Board of Commissioners for Foreign Missions, sponsored and sent more than 100 missionaries to the Kingdom of Hawaii between 1820 and 1850;

Whereas, on January 14, 1893, John L. Stevens (hereafter referred to in this Resolution as the "United States Minister"), the United States Minister assigned to the sovereign and independent Kingdom of Hawaii conspired with a small group of non-Hawaiian residents of the Kingdom of Hawaii, including citizens of the United States, to overthrow the indigenous and lawful Government of Hawaii;

Whereas, in pursuance of the conspiracy to overthrow the Government of Hawaii, the United States Minister and the naval representatives of the United States caused armed naval forces of the United States to invade the sovereign Hawaiian nation on January 16, 1893, and to position themselves near the Hawaiian Government buildings and the Iolani Palace to intimidate Queen Liliuokalani and her Government;

Whereas, on the afternoon of January 17, 1893, a Committee of Safety that represented the American and European sugar planters, descendants of missionaries, and financiers deposed the Hawaiian monarchy and proclaimed the establishment of a Provisional Government;

Whereas, the United States Minister thereupon extended diplomatic recognition to the Provisional Government that was formed by the conspirators without the consent of the Native Hawaiian people or the lawful Government of Hawaii and in violation of treaties between the two nations and of international law;

Whereas, soon thereafter, when informed of the risk of bloodshed with resistance, Queen Liliuokalani issued the following statement yielding her authority to the United States Government rather than to the Provisional Government:

"I Liliuokalani, by the Grace of God and under the Constitution of the Hawaiian Kingdom, Queen, do hereby solemnly protest against any and all acts done against myself and the Constitutional Government of the Hawaiian Kingdom by certain persons claiming to have established a Provisional Government of and for this Kingdom."

> "That I yield to the superior force of the United States of America whose Minister Plenipotentiary, His Excellency John L. Stevens, has caused United States troops to be landed a Honolulu and declared that he would support the Provisional Government."

> "Now to avoid any collision of armed forces, and perhaps the loss of life, I do this under protest and impelled by said force yield my authority until such time as the Government of the United States shall, upon facts being presented to it, undo the action of its representatives and reinstate me in the authority which I claim as the Constitutional Sovereign of the Hawaiian Islands."

Done at Honolulu this 17th day of January, A.D. 1893;

Whereas, without the active support and intervention by the United States diplomatic and military representatives, the insurrection against the

Appendix Two 113

Government of Queen Liliuokalani would have failed for lack of popular support and insufficient arms;

Whereas, on February 1, 1893, the United States Minister raised the American flag and proclaimed Hawaii to be a protectorate of the United States;

Whereas, the report of a Presidentially established investigation conducted by former Congressman James Blount into the events surrounding the insurrection and overthrow of January 17, 1893, concluded that the United States diplomatic and military representatives had abused their authority and were responsible for the change in government;

Whereas, as a result of this investigation, the United States Minister to Hawaii was recalled from his diplomatic post and the military commander of the United States armed forces stationed in Hawaii was disciplined and forced to resign his commission;

Whereas, in a message to Congress on December 18, 1893, President Grover Cleveland reported fully and accurately on the illegal acts of the conspirators, described such acts as an "act of war, committed with the participation of a diplomatic representative of the United States and without authority of Congress," and acknowledged that by such acts the government of a peaceful and friendly people was overthrown;

Whereas, President Cleveland further concluded that a "substantial wrong has thus been done which a due regard for our national character as well as the rights of the injured people requires we should endeavor to repair" and called for the restoration of the Hawaiian monarchy;

Whereas, the Provisional Government protested President Cleveland's call for the restoration of the monarchy and continued to hold state power and pursue annexation to the United States;

Whereas, the Provisional Government successfully lobbied the Committee on Foreign Relations of the Senate (hereafter referred to in this Resolution as the "Committee") to conduct a new investigation into the events surrounding the overthrow of the monarchy;

Whereas, the Committee and its chairman, Senator John Morgan, conducted hearings in Washington, D.C., from December 27, 1893, through February 26, 1894, in which members of the Provisional Government justified and condoned the actions of the United States Minister and recommended annexation of Hawaii;

Whereas, although the Provisional Government was able to obscure the role of the United States in the illegal overthrow of the Hawaiian monarchy, it was unable to rally the support from two-thirds of the Senate needed to ratify a treaty of annexation;

Whereas, on July 4, 1894, the Provisional Government declared itself to be the Republic of Hawaii;

Whereas, on January 24, 1895, while imprisoned in Iolani Palace, Queen Liliuokalani was forced by representatives of the Republic of Hawaii to officially abdicate her throne;

Whereas, in the 1896 United States Presidential election, William McKinley replaced Grover Cleveland;

Whereas, on July 7, 1898, as a consequence of the Spanish-American War, President McKinley signed the Newlands Joint Resolution that provided for the annexation of Hawaii;

Whereas, through the Newlands Resolution, the self-declared Republic of Hawaii ceded sovereignty over the Hawaiian Islands to the United States;

Whereas, the Republic of Hawaii also ceded 1,800,000 acres of crown, government and public lands of the Kingdom of Hawaii, without the consent of or compensation to the Native Hawaiian people of Hawaii or their sovereign government;

Whereas, the Congress, through the Newlands Resolution, ratified the cession, annexed Hawaii as part of the United States, and vested title to the lands in Hawaii in the United States;

Whereas, the Newlands Resolution also specified that treaties existing between Hawaii and foreign nations were to immediately cease and be replaced by United States treaties with such nations;

Whereas, the Newlands Resolution effected the transaction between the Republic of Hawaii and the United States Government;

Whereas, the indigenous Hawaiian people never directly relinquished their claims to their inherent sovereignty as a people or over their national lands to the United States, either through their monarchy or through a plebiscite or referendum;

Whereas, on April 30, 1900, President McKinley signed the Organic Act that provided a government for the territory of Hawaii and defined the political structure and powers of the newly established Territorial Government and its relationship to the United States;

Whereas, on August 21, 1959, Hawaii became the 50th State of the United States;

Whereas, the health and well-being of the Native Hawaiian people is intrinsically tied to their deep feelings and attachment to the land;

Whereas, the long-range economic and social changes in Hawaii over the nineteenth and early twentieth centuries have been devastating to the population and to the health and well-being of the Hawaiian people;

Appendix Two

Whereas, the Native Hawaiian people are determined to preserve, develop and transmit to future generations their ancestral territory, and their cultural identity in accordance with their own spiritual and traditional beliefs, customs, practices, language, and social institutions;

Whereas, in order to promote racial harmony and cultural understanding, the Legislature of the State of Hawaii has determined that the year 1993, should serve Hawaii as a year of special reflection on the rights and dignities of the Native Hawaiians in the Hawaiian and the American societies;

Whereas, the Eighteenth General Synod of the United Church of Christ in recognition of the denomination's historical complicity in the illegal overthrow of the Kingdom of Hawaii in 1893 directed the Office of the President of the United Church of Christ to offer a public apology to the Native Hawaiian people and to initiate the process of reconciliation between the United Church of Christ and the Native Hawaiians; and

Whereas, it is proper and timely for the Congress on the occasion of the impending one hundredth anniversary of the event, to acknowledge the historic significance of the illegal overthrow of the Kingdom of Hawaii, to express its deep regret to the Native Hawaiian people, and to support the reconciliation efforts of the State of Hawaii and the United Church of Christ with Native Hawaiians;

Now, therefore, be it

Resolved by the Senate and House of Representatives of the United States of America in Congress assembled,

SECTION 1. ACKNOWLEDGMENT AND APOLOGY.

The Congress -

1. on the occasion of the 100th anniversary of the illegal overthrow of the Kingdom of Hawaii on January 17, 1893, acknowledges the historical significance of this event which resulted in the suppression of the inherent sovereignty of the Native Hawaiian people;

2. recognizes and commends efforts of reconciliation initiated by the State of Hawaii and the United Church of Christ with Native Hawaiians;

3. apologizes to Native Hawaiians on behalf of the people of the United States for the overthrow of the Kingdom of Hawaii on

January 17, 1893 with the participation of agents and citizens of the United States, and the deprivation of the rights of Native Hawaiians to self-determination;

4. expresses its commitment to acknowledge the ramifications of the overthrow of the Kingdom of Hawaii, in order to provide a proper foundation for reconciliation between the United States and the Native Hawaiian people; and

5. urges the President of the United States to also acknowledge the ramifications of the overthrow of the Kingdom of Hawaii and to support reconciliation efforts between the United States and the Native Hawaiian people.

SEC. 2. DEFINITIONS.

As used in this Joint Resolution, the term "Native Hawaiians" means any individual who is a descendent of the aboriginal people who, prior to 1778, occupied and exercised sovereignty in the area that now constitutes the State of Hawaii.

SEC. 3. DISCLAIMER.

Nothing in this Joint Resolution is intended to serve as a settlement of any claims against the United States.
Approved November 23, 1993

Appendix Three

The Constitution of the State of Hawaii: Article XII, Selected Sections[1]

As Amended and in Force January 1, 2000

ARTICLE XII

Hawaiian Affairs, Hawaiian Homes Commission Act, Acceptance of Compact

Section 2. The State and its people do hereby accept, as a compact with the United States, or as conditions or trust provisions imposed by the United States, relating to the management and disposition of the Hawaiian home lands, the requirement that section 1 hereof be included in this constitution, in whole or in part, it being intended that the Act or acts of the Congress pertaining thereto shall be definitive of the extent and nature of such compact, conditions or trust provisions, as the case may be. The State and its people do further agree and declare that the spirit of the Hawaiian Homes Commission Act looking to the continuance of the Hawaiian homes projects for the further rehabilitation of the Hawaiian race shall be faithfully carried out.

ARTICLE XII

Hawaiian Affairs, Hawaiian Homes Commission Act, Traditional and Customary Rights

Section 7. The State reaffirms and shall protect all rights, customarily and traditionally exercised for subsistence, cultural and religious purposes and possessed by ahupua'a tenants who are descendants of native Hawaiians who inhabited the Hawaiian Islands prior to 1778, subject to the right of the State to regulate such rights.

Appendix Four
Indian Civil Rights Act of 1968: 25 USC 1302—1303[1]

1302. Constitutional Rights
No Indian tribe in exercising powers of self-government shall:

1. make or enforce any law prohibiting the free exercise of religion, or abridging the freedom of speech, or of the press, or the right of the people peaceably to assemble and to petition for a redress of grievances;

2. violate the right of the people to be secure in their persons, houses, papers, and effect against unreasonable search and seizures, nor issue warrants, but upon probably cause, supported by oath or affirmation, and particularly describing the place to be searched and the person or thing to be seized;

3. subject any person for the same offense to be twice put in jeopardy;

4. compel any person in any criminal case to be a witness against himself;

5. take any property for a public use without just compensation;

6. deny to any person in a criminal proceeding the right to a speedy and public trial, to be informed of the nature and cause of the accusation, to be confronted with the witnesses against him, to have compulsory process for obtaining witnesses in his favor, and at his own expense to have the assistance of counsel for his defense;

7. require excessive bail, impose excessive fines, inflict cruel and unusual punishments, and in no event impose for conviction of any one offense any penalty or punishment greater than imprisonment for a term of one year or a fine of $5,000 or both;

8. deny to any person within its jurisdiction the equal protection of its laws or deprive any person of liberty or property without due process of law;

9. pass any bill of attainder or ex post facto law; or

10. deny to any person accused of offense punishable by imprisonment the right, upon request, to a tribal by jury of not less than six persons.

1303. Habeas corpus

The privilege of the writ of habeas corpus shall be available to any person, in a court of the United States, to test the legality of his detention by order of an Indian tribe.

Appendix Five
Universal Declaration of Human Rights, Selected Articles[1]

Adopted and proclaimed by General Assembly resolution 217A (III) of 10 December 1948.

Article 15.
1. Everyone has the right to a nationality.
2. No one shall be arbitrarily deprived of his nationality nor denied the right to change his nationality.

Article 17.
1. Everyone has the right to own property alone as well as in association with others.
2. No one shall be arbitrarily deprived of his property.

Article 18.
1. Everyone has the right to freedom of thought, conscience and religion; this right includes freedom to change his religion or belief, and freedom, either alone or in community with others and in public or private, to manifest his religion or belief in teaching, practice, worship and observance.

Article 21.
1. Everyone has the right to take part in the government of his country, directly or through freely chosen representatives.
2. Everyone has the right of equal access to public service in his country.

3. The will of the people shall be the basis of the authority of government; this will shall be expressed in periodic and genuine elections which shall be by universal and equal suffrage and shall be held by secret vote or by equivalent free voting procedures.

Article 25.

1. Everyone has the right to a standard of living adequate for the health and well-being of himself and of his family, including food, clothing, housing and medical care and necessary social services, and the right to security in the event of unemployment, sickness, disability, widowhood, old age or other lack of livelihood in circumstances beyond his control.

2. Motherhood and childhood are entitled to special care and assistance. All children, whether born in or out of wedlock, shall enjoy the same social protection.

Notes

NOTES TO CHAPTER ONE

1. A more in depth exploration of indigenousness will follow in Chapter Three, "On Indigenousness."
2. The term American Indians applies to indigenous peoples in the lower-48 states only. Alaskan Natives and Native Hawaiians are referred to separately as they have a distinct legal status and experience as compared to American Indians. The term Native American includes Alaskan Natives, Native Hawaiians, and American Indians (members of tribes originally living in the area of the continental United States). Throughout the book, the term Native American bears this meaning, and the term American Indian applies specifically to tribes of the continental United States.
3. The case of the Inuit in Canada who were willing to accept governing power over the newly created Nunavut Territories stops short of becoming a state. Kymlicka (1995) suggests that it would not be possible for all nations to become states. Acknowledging this, it is a good idea to soften the edges of Weber's definition, allowing communities that seek to achieve greater self-governance—that stops short of statehood—to be included.
4. Looking at 132 political bodies that are, by consensus, deemed states (in 1971), Connor (1994 [1978]) finds that only 12 states (9.1%) are nation-states. The remaining 120 bodies contain various proportions of the state population consisting of only one nation or potential nation. Connor groups them in four categories and the distribution is as follows: "more than 90% of the population of one nation or potential nation" 25 states (18.9%), "75%-89% of the population of one nation or potential nation" 25 states (18.9%), "50%-74% of the population of one nation or potential nation" 31 states (23.5%), "less than half of the population of one nation or potential nation" 39 states (29.5%). The modal group of this population of states has less than half of its population in one national group. Even the nation-states and the "more than 90% . . ." groups combined do not outnumber this modal group.

5. This is the wording in the treaty which Boldt's decision upholds. Regarding the harvest of shellfish and access rights, this Boldt Decision is especially relevant here (although it includes fishing and hunting more generally). Under the Boldt Decision, Indians can harvest shellfish from the tidal flats that homeowners argued was private property. It only excludes the right to planted shellfish beds.

NOTES TO CHAPTER THREE

1. As an example, other tribes often sue American Indian tribes applying for federal acknowledgement. Existing federally recognized tribes challenge the authenticity of the identity claims of petitioning tribes aggressively.

NOTES TO CHAPTER FOUR

1. The Trasks are one of the islands' most persistent political clans (Heckathorn 1998 [1992]). Hanauani -Kay is a professor at the University of Hawaii, Mililani heads *Ka Lāhui* Hawai'i, David (Hanauani-Kay and Mililani's uncle) was the president of the Hawai'i Government Employees' Association for years, and grandfather David Trask was a territorial legislator (Heckathorn 1998 [1992]). Haunani-Kay has written extensively on the Native Hawaiian experience, and Mililani has authored a few pieces as well. I include this note as a contextual detail.
2. *Haole* means "white foreigner" in Hawaiian (Trask, H. 1999: footnote on p. 4).
3. Wallerstein (2000) describes this phenomenon in Africa. Similar forces are at work in Hawaii.
4. The nation-to-nation status may be an ideal that does not exist. This is the case for American Indians, who remain wards of the government, and at the same time are supposed to have a government-to-government relationship with the United States. There is no equality, which is implied by the nation-to-nation status. In readings regarding the Hawaiian movement (especially Trask, H. 1999 and Hartwell 1996), the authors state that one goal of the Hawaiian movement is attaining a nation-to-nation relationship with the United States government. I do not wish to put words in the author's mouths here, and for this reason I will not dispute the viability of such a proposition for the Hawaiians. But it is important to acknowledge that the operationalization of "nation-to-nation" might not include the implied freedoms.
5. Sovereignty is a legal and political concept. By the lay understanding, "sovereignty is a legal concept that means the legitimate and recognized governmental power over people and territory" (Cooper n.d.: 3). The principle of sovereignty has a collective character, which is concerned with human beings not only as sole autonomous actors, but also as social people engaged in the constitution and functioning of communities (Anaya 1996). The State is sovereign to the extent that it has extracted coercion

from private property and has acquired an organization that allows it to express and enforce the will of the State (Commons 1900). The simple legal definition of sovereignty is: "the inherent right or power to govern" (Canby 1988:66).
6. Two lawsuits have been garnering attention lately, both arguing that rights given to Native Hawaiians by the state discriminate against non-Native Hawaiians. One case, Rice v. Ceytano, went in favor of the non-Native Hawaiians. This case found that non-Natives should be allowed to vote for members of the Board of Trustees of the Office of Hawaiian affairs (and that to prohibit non-natives from participating was discriminatory). The other case is still being heard. Barrett is the plaintiff in this case, and he argues that the Office of Hawaiian Affairs is discriminatory because it serves only Native Hawaiians.
7. These planks include: an apology by the United States government to Native Hawaiians; a land and natural resource base; recognition of the Native Hawaiian government with authority over the territory; guarantees of beach access, protections of religious practices and sites, and fishing, hunting, and gathering rights; an appropriate cash payment (Heckathorn 1998 [1988]).

NOTES TO CHAPTER FIVE

1. Hybridity results when two or more cultures are incorporated to create a new cultural identity. The identities are not assimilated or altered independently, but instead elements of the cultures are incorporated to create a new hybrid culture. The result: a third identity emerges which is not the same as the independent parts. Further detail on defining this concept is below within the body of Chapter Five.

NOTES TO CHAPTER SIX

1. The Inter-American Commission on Human Rights approved the Proposed American Declaration of the Rights of Indigenous Peoples (1997) on February 26, 1997 (Anaya 1996).
2. The UN Working Group on Indigenous Populations agreed upon the UN Draft Declaration on the Rights of Indigenous Peoples at its eleventh session in July 1993. The UN Subcommission on Prevention of Discrimination and Protection of Minorities adopted it in August 1994.
3. This doctrine was adopted on 27 June 1989 by the general conference of the International Labour Organization, the Convention Concerning Indigenous and Tribal Peoples in Independent Countries. This conference is also known as Convention Number 169. According to Article 36 of the document, this Convention revises the Indigenous and Tribal Populations Convention, 1957. The United States has not ratified this doctrine. As of early 2003, 17 countries have ratified Convention Number 169, including Mexico (ratified on 5 September 1990). This document

can be viewed in its full format online at http://ilolex.ilo.ch:1567/english/conv.disp1.htm.
4. The Declaration of Principles on the Rights of Indigenous Peoples (1987) was prepared for the fourth session of the United Nations Working Group on Indigenous Populations in 1985 and finalized in 1987.
5. United Nations Educational, Scientific and Cultural Organization's Universal Draft Declaration on Cultural Diversity was adopted in 2001. The document was written to illustrate the organization's commitment "to the full implementation of the human rights and fundamental freedoms proclaimed in the Universal Declaration of Human Rights and other universally recognized legal instruments, such as the two International Covenants of 1966 relating respectively to civil and political rights and to economic, social and cultural rights" (Universal Draft Declaration on Cultural Diversity, opening lines 2001). UNESCO views the protection of culture as a matter of justice and liberty for all.
6. The European Parliament adopted the Resolution on Action Required Internationally To Provide Effective Protection for Indigenous Peoples in its plenary session 1994.
7. The United Nations Declaration on the Granting of Independence to Colonial Countries and Peoples was adopted by the United Nations General Assembly on 14 December 1960.
8. The United Nations International Covenant on Civil and Political Rights is dated 1966, and was entered into force on 23 March 1976.
9. In 1977, indigenous participants at the Non-Governmental Organization Conference on Discrimination Against Indigenous Populations wrote The Draft Declaration of Principles for the Defense of the Indigenous Nations and Peoples of the Western Hemisphere.
10. It is not clear if this bill applies to Native Hawaiians. I will discuss this in further detail below.
11. Applying this argument to American Indians would involve an entirely different argument. For more on that topic, see Deloria and Wilkins (1999). The difference between Native Hawaiians and American Indians is also discussed in Chapter One.
12. I was unable to find an English version of this document. Using an online translation service, Babelfish, I was able to convert the document to English. Although this software was not flawless in its translation (issues seemed to arise in the subjunctive tense and the verb "to be" was often not translated), the basic concepts seem to be communicated. When an English version of this document is available a more in-depth analysis can be performed.

NOTES TO APPENDIX ONE

1. This text is a transcription of the first ten Amendments to the Constitution in their original form. These amendments were ratified December 15, 1791, and form what is known as the "Bill of Rights." (*Source*: http://

www.archives.gov/exhibit_hall/charters_of_freedom/bill_of_rights/amendments_1–10.html)

NOTES TO APPENDIX TWO

1. (*Source*: http://www.hawaii-nation.org/publawall.html)

NOTES TO APPENDIX THREE

1. (*Source*: http://www.hawaii.gov/lrb/con/conart12.html)

NOTES TO APPENDIX FOUR

1. (*Source*: http://thorpe.ou.edu/AKtribalct/appendix_a.html)

NOTES TO APPENDIX FIVE

1. (*Source*: http://www.un.org/Overview/rights.html. Reprinted with permission.)

Bibliography

Abi-Saab, Georges. 1994. "The Changing World Order and the International Legal Order: The Structural Evolution of International Law Beyond the State-Centric Model." Pp. 439–461 in *Global Transformation: Challenges to the State System* edited by Yoshikazo Sakamoto. Tokyo, Japan: United Nations University Press.
Adamski, Mary. 2002. "Kawaiahao's potential leader comes with high regard." *Honolulu Star Bulletin* 26 October 2002. http://starbulletin.com/2002/10/26/features/story1.html (26 October 2002).
Agustín, Miguel and Edgar Cortéz. 2001. "The Indigenous Rights and Culture Law and Peace Process." *Global Exchange*. 27 April 2001. http://www.globalexchange.org/campaigns/mexico/news/042701.html (22 April 2003).
Akaka, Moanikeala. Trustee, Office of Hawaiian Affairs. 1989. "United Nations Working Group on Indigenous Populations." *Fourth World Documentation Project*. The Center for Word Indigenous Studies. 3 August 1989. http://www.halcyon.com/pub/FWDP/Oceania/hawaii.txt (2 May 2001).
Alger, Chadwick F. 1997. "Transnational Social Movements, World Politics, and Global Governance" pp. 260–275 in *Transnational Social Movements and Global Politics: Solidarity Beyond the State.* Edited by Jackie Smith, Charles Chatfield, and Ron Pagnucco. Syracuse, NY: Syracuse University Press.
Aluli, Noa Emmett and Davianna Pomaika'I McGregor. 1994. "The Healing of Kaho'olawe." Pp. 197–208 in *Hawaii: Return to Nationhood.* Edited by Ulla Hasager and Jonathan Friedman. Copenhagen, Denmark: International Working Group for Indigenous Affairs.
Anaya, S. James. 1996. *Indigenous Peoples in International Law.* New York: Oxford University Press.
An-Na'im, Abdullahi Ahmed. 2001. "Human Rights." Pp. 86–99 in *The Blackwell Companion to Sociology* edited by Judith R. Blau. Malden, MA: Blackwell Publishers Inc.
Anderson, Benedict. 1991. *Imagined Communities.* London, UK: Verso.
Aoude, Ibrahim G. 1999. "Hawai'i: Strategic Considerations for Social Struggles." Pp. 284–300 in *Social Process in Hawai'i*. Volume 39.

———. 2001. "Policy of Globalization and Globalization of Policy." Pp. xi-xxvii in *Social Process in Hawai'i*. Volume 39.
Appadurai, Arjun. 1998. *Modernity at Large: Cultural Dimensions of Globalization*. Minneapolis, MN: University of Minnesota Press.
Aristotle. 1968. *The Politics of Aristotle*. Translated by Ernest Baker. Oxford, UK: Clarendon Press.
Armstrong, John. 1994 [1982]. "Nations Before Nationalism." Pp. 140–147 in *Nationalism* edited by John Hutchinson and Anthony D. Smith. Oxford, UK: Oxford University Press.
Babbie, Earl. 1988. *The Sociological Spirit*. Belmont, CA: Wadsworth Publishing Company.
Badie, Bertrand and Pierre Birnbaum. 1983. *The Sociology of the State*. Translated by Arthur Goldhammer. Chicago, IL: University of Chicago Press.
Balakrishnan, Gopal. 1996. *Mapping the Nation*. London, UK: Verso.
Balibar, Etienne and Immanuel Wallerstein. 1991. *Race, Nation, Class: Ambiguous Identities*. London, UK: Verso.
Bamyeh, Mohammed A. 2000. *The Ends of Globalization*. Minneapolis, MN: University of Minnesota Press.
Barcham, Manuhuia. 2000. "(De)Constructing the Politics of Indigeneity." Pp. 137–151 in *Political Theory and the Rights of Indigenous Peoples*. Edited by Duncan Ivison, Paul Patton, and Will Sanders. Cambridge, UK: Cambridge University Press.
Bauman, Zygmunt. 1998. *Globalization: The Human Consequences*. New York: Columbia University Press.
Beck, Ulrich. 1999. *World Risk Society*. Malden, MA: Polity Press.
———. 2000. *What is Globalization?* Translated by Patrick Camiller. Malden, MA: Polity Press.
Benhabib, Seyla. 2002. *The Claims of Culture: Equality and Diversity in the Global Era*. Princeton, NJ: Princeton University Press.
Berger, Peter L. and Thomas Luckmann. 1967. *The Social Construction of Reality*. Garden City, NY: Anchor Books.
Bern, John and Susan Dodds. 2000. "On the Plurality of Interests: Aboriginal Self-government and Land Rights." Pp. 163–179 in *Political Theory and the Rights of Indigenous Peoples*. Edited by Duncan Ivison, Paul Patton, and Will Sanders. Cambridge, UK: Cambridge University Press.
Bhabha, Homi K. 1994. *The Location of Culture*. London, UK: Routledge.
Blaisdell, Kekuni and Noreen Mokuau. 1994. "Kanaka Maoli, Indigenous Hawaiians." Pp. 49–67 in *Hawaii: Return to Nationhood*. Edited by Ulla Hasager and Jonathan Friedman. Copenhagen, Denmark: International Working Group for Indigenous Affairs.
Blau, Judith R. and Eric S. Brown. 2001. "Du Bois and Diasporic Identity: The *Veil* and *Unveiling* Project." Pp. 219–233 in *Sociological Theory*. 19:2.
Boli, John and George M. Thomas. 1997. "World Culture in the World Polity: A Century of International Non-Governmental Organizations" pp. 171–190 in *American Sociological Review* Volume 62, Number 2.
———. 1999. *Constructing World Culture: International Nongovernmental Organizations Since 1875*. Stanford, CA: Stanford University Press.

Brown Thompson, Karen. 2004. "Women's Rights are Human Rights." Pp. 96–122 in *Restructuring World Politics: Transnational Social Movements, Networks, and Norms.* Edited by Sanjeev Khagram, James V. Riker, and Kathryn Sikkink. Minneapolis, MN: University of Minnesota Press.

Brunn, Stanley D. 1999. "Geopolitical Information and Communications in the Twenty-First Century" pp. 292–318 in *Reordering the World: Geopolitical Perspectives on the 21st Century* Second Edition. Edited by George J. Demko and William B. Wood. Boulder, CO: Westview Press.

Bulter, Judith, Ernesto Laclau and Slavoj Zizek. 2000. *Contingency, Hegemony, Universality: Contemporary Dialogues on the Left.* London, UK: Verso.

Calhoun, Craig. 2000 [1993]. ""New Social Movements" of the Early Nineteenth Century." Pp. 129–154 in *Readings in Contemporary Political Sociology.* Edited by Kate Nash. Malden, MA: Blackwell Publishers.

Canby, Jr., William C. 1988. *American Indian Law in a Nutshell.* St. Paul, MN: West Publishing Co.

Castanha, Anthony. 1996. "The Hawaiian Sovereignty Movement: Roles of and Impacts on Non-Hawaiians: Chapter 3 A History of the Hawaiian Sovereignty Movement." From *The Hawaiian Sovereignty Movement: Roles of and Impacts on Non-Hawaiians.* M.A. thesis, University of Hawaii, August 1996. http://www.hookele.com/non-hawaiians/chapter3.html (28 February 2001).

Chatfield, Charles. 1997. "Intergovernmental and Nongovernmental Associations to 1945" pp. 19–41 in *Transnational Social Movements and Global Politics: Solidarity Beyond the State.* Edited by Jackie Smith, Charles Chatfield, and Ron Pagnucco. Syracuse, NY: Syracuse University Press.

Chatterjee, Partha. 1993. *Nationalist Thought and the Colonial World: A Derivative Discourse.* Minneapolis, MN: University of Minnesota Press.

Cheru, Fantu. 2000. "The Local Dimensions of Global Reform." Pp. 119–132 in *Global Futures: Shaping Globalization.* Edited by Jan Nederveen Pieterse. London, UK: Zed Books.

Clifford, James. 1997 [1994]. "Diasporas." Pp. 283–290 in *The Ethnicity Reader: Nationalism, Multiculturalism, and Migration.* Edited by Montserrat Guibernau and John Rex. Cambridge, UK: Polity Press.

Cohen, Bernard P. 1989. *Developing Sociological Knowledge: Theory and Method, Second Edition.* Chicago, IL: Nelson-Hall Inc.

Commons, John R. 1899. "A Sociological View of Sovereignty. I." Pp. 1–15 in *American Journal of Sociology.* 5:1.

———. 1900. "A Sociological View of Sovereignty. VIII." Pp. 67–89 in *American Journal of Sociology.* 6:1.

Connolly, William E. 2000 [1989]. "Identity and Difference in Global Politics." Pp. 336–347 in *Readings in Contemporary Political Sociology* edited by Kate Nash. Malden, MA: Blackwell Publishers.

Connor, Walker. 1994 [1978]. "A Nation is a Nation, is a State, is an Ethnic Group, is a. . . ." Pp. 36–46 in *Nationalism* edited by John Hutchinson and Anthony D. Smith. Oxford, UK: Oxford University Press.

Constitution of the State of Hawaii (as Amended and in Force January 1, 2000). 1978. Text Downloaded from www.hawaii.gov/lrb/con/ (4 March 2003).

Constitution of the United States of Mexico. 1917 (with amendments dated to 1968). Translated from Constitución Política de los Estados Unidos Mexicanos, Trigésima Quinta Edición. 1967. Washington, D.C.: Pan American Union, General Secretariat, Organization of American States. 1968. http://www.ilstu.edu/class/hist263/docs/1917const.html (10 February 2003).
Cooper, David E. K. 1999. "The Quest for Sovereignty in the Pacific." *The Pacific American Foundation.* The Pacific American Foundation. 5 April 1999. http://www.thepaf.org/info/QFS.htm (2 May 2001).
Corbett, J. Angelo. 2000. "Secession and Native Americans." Pp. 7–14 in *Peace Review,* 12:1.
Cornell, Stephen E. 1988. *The Return of the Native: American Indian Political Resurgence.* New York: Oxford University Press.
Corntassel, Jeff J. and Tomas Hopkins Primeau. 1995. "Indigenous "Sovereignty" and International Law: Revised Strategies for Pursuing "Self-Determination." Pp. 343–365 in *Human Rights Quarterly* 17:2.
Craven, Matthew. 2002. *Continuity of the Hawaiian Kingdom, Reader in International Law.* London, UK: SOAS, University of London.
Daws, Gavan. 1968. *Shoal of Time: A History of the Hawaiian Islands.* Honolulu, HI: University of Hawaii Press.
Deloria, Jr. Vine and David E. Wilkins. 1999. *Tribes, Treaties and Constitutional Tribulations.* Austin, TX: University of Texas Press.
DePledge, Derrick. 2002. "Hawaiians advised to 'define' their goals." *Honolulu Advertiser* 11 September 2002. http://thehonoluluadvertiser.com/article/2002/Sep/11/ln/ln05a.html/. (5 October 2002).
Deutsch, Karl W. 1994 [1966]. "Nationalism and Social Communication." Pp. 26–29 in *Nationalism* edited by John Hutchinson and Anthony D. Smith. Oxford, UK: Oxford University Press.
Du Bois, W. E. B. 1903. *The Souls of Black Folk.* Chicago, IL: A.C. McClurg & Co. Cambridge, MA: University Press John Wilson and Son. Bartleby.com, 1999. www.bartleby.com/114/. (26 December 2001, 8 April 2003).
Dudley, Michael Kioni and Keoni Kealoha Agard. 1993. *A Call for Hawaiian Sovereignty.* Honolulu Hawai'i: Nā Kāne O Ka Malo Press.
Eriksen, Thomas Hylland. 1997 [1993]. "Ethnicity, race and nation." Pp. 33–42 in *The Ethnicity Reader: Nationalism, Multiculturalism, and Migration.* Edited by Montserrat Guibernau and John Rex. Cambridge, UK: Polity Press.
Evans, Peter B., Dietrich Rueschemeyer, and Theda Skocpol. 1985. *Bringing the State Back In.* Cambridge, UK: Cambridge University Press.
"Experts look to Australia's Aborigines for weather help." 2003. *CNN.com/Science & Space.* 19 March 2003. http://www.cnn.com/2003/TECH/science/03/18/offbeat.weather.aborigines.reut/index.html (19 March 2002).
Falk, Richard. 2000. "Humane Governance for the World: Reviving the Quest." Pp. 23–39 in *Global Futures: Shaping Globalization.* Edited by Jan Nederveen Pieterse. London, UK: Zed Books.
Field-Grace, Sondra. 1994. "Anahola—Taro-Roots Practice Self-Determination." Pp. 210–213 in *Hawaii: Return to Nationhood.* Edited by Ulla Hasager and Jonathan Friedman. Copenhagen, Denmark: International Working Group for Indigenous Affairs.

Finnemore, Martha and Kathryn Sikkink. 1998. "International Norm Dynamics and Political Change." Pp. 887–917 in *International Organization*, 52:4.

Fraser, Nancy and Linda Gordon. 1998 [1992]. *Contract versus Charity: Why is There No Social Citizenship in the United States?* Pp. 113–127 in *The Citizenship Debates*. Edited by Gershon Shafir. Minneapolis, MN: University of Minnesota Press.

Friedman, Thomas L. 1999. "Indigenous Struggles and the Discreet Charm of the Bourgeoisie." Pp. 391–411 in *Journal of World Systems Research*, 5:2.

Fujimori, Leila. 2002. "Leasehold land bill draws native Hawaiian protest: Protesters compare the Council measure to "land grabbing." *Honolulu Star Bulletin*. 8 September 2002. http://starbulletin.com/2002/09/08/news/story11.html (8 September 2002).

Gandhi, Leela. 1998. *Postcolonial Theory*. New York: Columbia University Press.

Geertz, Clifford. 1994 [1963]. "Primordial and Civic Ties." Pp. 29–34 in *Nationalism* edited by John Hutchinson and Anthony D. Smith. Oxford, UK: Oxford University Press.

Gellner, Ernest. 1983. *Nations and Nationalism*. Ithaca, NY: Cornell University Press.

General Command of the Zapatista National Liberation Army. 2002 [1993]. First Declaration from the Lacandón Jungle. Pp. 217-.220 in *The Zapatista Reader* edited by Tom Hayden. New York: Thunder's Mouth Press.

———. 2002 [1996]. Fourth Declaration from the Lacandón Jungle. Pp. 239–250 in *The Zapatista Reader* edited by Tom Hayden. New York: Thunder's Mouth Press.

———. 2002 [1994]. Second Declaration from the Lacandón Jungle. Pp. 221–231 in *The Zapatista Reader* edited by Tom Hayden. New York: Thunder's Mouth Press.

———. 2002 [1995]. Third Declaration from the Lacandón Jungle. Pp. 231- 239 in *The Zapatista Reader* edited by Tom Hayden. New York: Thunder's Mouth Press.

Getches, David H., Charles F. Wilkinson, and Robert A. Williams, Jr. 1993. *Federal Indian Law: Cases and Materials*. St. Paul, MN: West Publishing Co.

Giddens, Anthony. 1994 [1985]. "The Nation as Power-Container." Pp. 34–35 in *Nationalism* edited by John Hutchinson and Anthony D. Smith. Oxford, UK: Oxford University Press.

———. 2000. *Runaway World*. New York: Routledge.

Gill, Stephen. 1994. "Structural Change and Global Political Economy: Globalizing Elites and the Emerging World Order." Pp. 169–199 in *Global Transformation: Challenges to the State System* edited by Yoshikazo Sakamoto. Tokyo, Japan: United Nations University Press.

Gilroy, Paul. 1993. *The Black Atlantic: Modernity and Double Consciousness*. Cambridge, MA: Harvard University Press.

Giordano, Al. 2001. "Zapatistas on the March." *The Nation*, April 9, pp. 6–7, 26.

Gomes, L. Ku'umeaaloha. 1994. "Malama I Kekahi I Kekahi." Pp. 68–70 in *Hawaii: Return to Nationhood*. Edited by Ulla Hasager and Jonathan Friedman. Copenhagen, Denmark: International Working Group for Indigenous Affairs.

Goonatilake, Susantha. 1995. "The Self Wandering Between Cultural Localization and Globalization." Pp. 225–239 in *The Decolonization of Imagination: Culture, Knowledge and Power* edited by Jan Nederveen Pieterse and Bhikhu Parekh. London: Zed Books Ltd.

Greenfeld, Liah. 1994 [1992]. "Types of European Nationalism." Pp. 165–171 in *Nationalism* edited by John Hutchinson and Anthony D. Smith. Oxford, UK: Oxford University Press.

Greider, William. 1997. *One World, Ready or Not: The Manic Logic of Global Capitalism.* New York: Simon and Schuster.

Griffin, Keith. 2000. "Culture and Economic Growth: The State and Globalization." Pp. 189–202 in *Global Futures: Shaping Globalization.* Edited by Jan Nederveen Pieterse. London, UK: Zed Books.

Guehenno, Jean-Marie. 1995. *The End of the Nation-State.* Minneapolis, MN: University of Minnesota Press.

Guibernau, Montserrat. 1999. *Nations Without States: Political Communities in a Global Age.* Cambridge, UK: Polity Press.

Gutmann, Amy. 2001. "Introduction." Pp. vii-xxviii in *Human Rights as Politics and Idolatry*, edited by Amy Gutmann. Princeton, NJ: Princeton University Press.

Hall, Stuart. 1997. "The Local and the Global: Globalization and Ethnicity." Pp. 19–39 in *Culture, Globalization and the World-System*, edited by Anthony D. King. Minneapolis, MN: University of Minnesota Press.

Halualani, Rona Tamiko. 1997. "A Sovereign Nation's Functional Mythic Discourses." Pp. 89–121 in *Politics, Communication, and Culture, Volume XX.* Edited by Alberto Gonzalez and Dolores V. Tanno. Thousand Oaks, CA: Sage Publications.

Hardt, Michael and Antonio Negri. 2001. *Empire.* Cambridge, MA: Harvard University Press.

Hartwell, Jay. 1996. *Nā Mamo: Hawaiian People Today.* Honolulu, HI: 'Ai Pōhaku Press.

Hasager, Ulla. 1999. "Indigenous Rights, Praxis, and Social Institutions." Pp. 155–180 in *Social Process in Hawai'i.* Volume 39.

———and Jonathan Friedman. 1994. "Hawai'i Now." Pp. 7–11 in *Hawaii: Return to Nationhood.* Edited by Ulla Hasager and Jonathan Friedman. Copenhagen, Denmark: International Working Group for Indigenous Affairs.

Hawkins, Darren. 2004. "Human Rights Norms and Networks in Authoritarian Chile." Pp. 47–70 in *Restructuring World Politics: Transnational Social Movements, Networks, and Norms.* Edited by Sanjeev Khagram, James V. Riker, and Kathryn Sikkink. Minneapolis, MN: University of Minnesota Press.

Hayden, Tom, Editor. 2002. *The Zapatista Reader.* New York: Thunder's Mouth Press.

Hechter, Michael and Elizabeth Borland. 2001. "National Self-Determination: The Emergence of an Institutional Norm." pp. 186–233 in *Social Norms.* Edited by Michael Hechter and Karl-Dieter Opp. New York: Russell Sage Foundation.

Bibliography

———and Margaret Levi. 1994 [1979]. "Ethno-Regional Movements in the West." Pp. 184–195 in *Nationalism* edited by John Hutchinson and Anthony D. Smith. Oxford, UK: Oxford University Press.

Heckathorn, Bruce. 1998 [1992]. "Islander of the Year." Pp. 338–347 in *Hawaii Chronicles II: Contemporary Island History*. Edited by Bob Dye. Honolulu, HI: University of Hawaii Press.

———. 1998 [1988]. "The Native Hawaiian Nation: The Hottest Political Issue of the 1990s." Pp. 324–337 in *Hawaii Chronicles II: Contemporary Island History*. Edited by Bob Dye. Honolulu, HI: University of Hawaii Press.

Held, David, Anthony McGrew, David Goldblatt, and Jonathan Perraton. 1999. *Global Transformations: Politics, Economics, and Culture*. Stanford, CA: Stanford University Press.

Hettne, Bjorn. 1994. "The Regional Factor in the Formation of a New World Order." Pp. 134–166 in *Global Transformation: Challenges to the State System* edited by Yoshikazo Sakamoto. Tokyo, Japan: United Nations University Press.

Hobbes, Thomas. 1962. *Leviathan*. Edited by Michael Oakeshott with an introduction by Richard Peters. New York: Collier Books.

Hobsbawm, Eric. 1994 [1990]. "The Rise of Ethno-Linguistic Nationalisms." Pp. 177–184 in *Nationalism* edited by John Hutchinson and Anthony D. Smith. Oxford, UK: Oxford University Press.

Hoppe, Hans-Hermann. 1996. "Small is Beautiful and Efficient: The Case for Secession." Pp. 95–101 in *Telos*, 107:Spring.

Howard, Rhoda E. 1995. *Human Rights and the Search for Community*. Boulder, CO: Westview Press.

———. 1995. "Human Rights and the Search for Community." Pp. 1–8 in *Journal of Peace Reserch* 32:1.

———and Jack Donnelly. 1986. "Human Dignity, Human Rights, and Political Regimes." Pp. 801–817 in *The American Political Science Review* 80:3.

Ignatieff, Michael. 2001. "Dignity and Agency." Pp. 161–173 in *Human Rights as Politics and Idolatry*, edited by Amy Gutmann. Princeton, NJ: Princeton University Press.

———. 2001. "Human Rights as Idolatry." Pp. 53–98 in *Human Rights as Politics and Idolatry*, edited by Amy Gutmann. Princeton, NJ: Princeton University Press.

———. 2001. "Human Rights as Politics." Pp. 3–52 in *Human Rights as Politics and Idolatry*, edited by Amy Gutmann. Princeton, NJ: Princeton University Press.

International Labour Organisation. 1989. *Convention (No 169) Concerning Indigenous and Tribal Peoples in Independent Countries*. International Labour Conference, Geneva, 76th Session.

Ito, Karen L. 1999. *Lady Friends: Hawaiian Ways and the Ties That Define*. Ithaca, NY: Cornell University Press.

"Ka Ho'okolokolonui Kanaka Maoli: The People's International Tribunal Hawai'i, 1993." 1994. Pp. 288–296 in *Hawaii: Return to Nationhood*. Edited by Ulla Hasager and Jonathan Friedman. Copenhagen, Denmark: International Working Group for Indigenous Affairs.

Ka Pae'aina o Hawai'i Loa (United Independence Statement). 1999. Produced at a meeting convened by Kanaka United For Action, with the support of the Hawai'i Ecumenical Coalition and Ke Kia'i. *Hawai'i Independent and Sovereign*. http://www.hawaii-nation.org/united-independence.html (7 February 2001 and 3 May 2003).

Kame'eleihiwa, Lilikala. 1994. "Ua Mau Ke Ea o Ka 'Aina i Ka Pono." Pp. 36–43 in *Hawaii: Return to Nationhood*. Edited by Ulla Hasager and Jonathan Friedman. Copenhagen, Denmark: International Working Group for Indigenous Affairs.

Kellas, James G. 1998. *The Politics of Nationalism and Ethnicity, Second Edition*. New York: St. Martin's Press.

Kellner, Douglas. 2002. "Theorizing Globalization." Pp. 285–304 in *Sociological Theory*. 20:3.

Kelly, John/Maka'ainana Media. 1994. "Look What Happened to Waikiki." Pp. 254–255 in *Hawaii: Return to Nationhood*. Edited by Ulla Hasager and Jonathan Friedman. Copenhagen, Denmark: International Working Group for Indigenous Affairs.

Kent, Noel Jacob. 1999. "Notes on Globalization as Salvation: The Myth That Never Dies." Pp. 275–283 in *Social Process in Hawai'i*. Volume 39.

Khagram, Sanjeev, James V. Riker, and Kathryn Sikkink. 2004. "From Santiago to Seattle: Transnational Advocacy Groups Restructuring World Politics." Pp. 3–23 in *Restructuring World Politics: Transnational Social Movements, Networks, and Norms*. Edited by Sanjeev Khagram, James V. Riker, and Kathryn Sikkink. Minneapolis, MN: University of Minnesota Press.

Kilminster, Richard. 1997. "Globalization as an Emergent Concept." Pp. 257–283 in *The Limits of Globalization: Cases and Arguments*. Edited by Alan Scott. London, UK: Routledge.

Knight, David B. 1999. "People Together Yet Apart: Rethinking Territory, Sovereignty, and Identities" pp. 209–226 in *Reordering the World: Geopolitical Perspectives on the 21st Century* Second Edition. Edited by George J. Demko and William B. Wood. Boulder, CO: Westview Press.

Kohler, Gernot. 2003. "Comparative advantage: Comparative exploitation." *Asia Times Online*. 29 January 2003. http://www.atimes.com/atimes/Global_Economy/EA29Dj02.html (29 January 2003).

Krasner, Stephen D. 1999. "Globalization and Sovereignty." Pp. 34–52 in *States and Sovereignty in the Global Economy*. Edited by David A. Smith, Dorothy J. Solinger, and Steven C. Topik. London, UK: Routledge.

Kuykendall, Ralph S. and A. Grove Day. 1948. *Hawaii: A History*. New York: Prentice Hall, Inc.

Kymlicka, Will. 1995. *Multicultural Citizenship*. Oxford, UK: Oxford University Press.

Lam, Maivan Clech. 1992. "Making Room for Peoples at the United Nations: Thoughts Provoked by Indigenous Claims to Self-Determination." Pp. 603–622 in *Cornell International Law Journal*. Volume 23.

Levi, Margaret. 1988. *Of Rule and Revenue*. Berkeley, CA: University of California Press.

"Ley de Derechos y Cultura Indígena" (Law of Rights and Indigenous Culture). 1999. Publicacion Estatal: Secretaria de Gobierno Direccion de Asunto

Juridicos Departmento de Gobernacion. *Centro De Investigaciones Económicas y Políticas de Acción Comunitaria.* http://www.ciepac.org/Leyes/Derechos%20 y%20Cultura%20Ind%EDgena.ht Translated with Atlavista.com's *Babel Fish Translation* http://babelfish.altavista.com/. (12 February 2002).

Lipset, Seymour Martin. 1963. *The First New Nation: The United States in Historical and Comparative Perspective.* Garden City, NY: Anchor Books.

———. 1994 [1959]. *Political Man: The Social Bases of Politics.* Baltimore, MD: The Johns Hopkins University Press.

Livingston, Donald W. 1998. "The Very Idea of Secession." Pp. 38–48 in *Society*, 35:5.

Lo, Ming-cheng M. 2002. *Doctors Within Borders: Profession, Ethnicity, and Modernity in Colonial Taiwan.* Berkeley: University of California Press.

Lukes, Steven. 1974. *Power: A Radical Review.* London, UK: Macmillan.

Maaka, Roger and Augie Fleras. 2000. "Engaging with Indigeneity: Tino Rangatiratanga in Aotearoa." Pp. 89–109 in *Political Theory and the Rights of Indigenous Peoples.* Edited by Duncan Ivison, Paul Patton, and Will Sanders. Cambridge, UK: Cambridge University Press.

Maiguashca, Bice. 1994. "The Transnational Indigenous Movement in a Changing World Order." Pp. 356–382 in *Global Transformation: Challenges to the State System* edited by Yoshikazo Sakamoto. Tokyo, Japan: United Nations University Press.

Mallon, Florencia E. 1996 [1992]. "Indigenous Peoples and the State in Latin America." Pp. 291–294 in *Ethnicity*, edited by John Hutchinson and Anthony D. Smith. Oxford, UK: Oxford University Press.

Malo, David. 1951. *Hawaiian Antiquities.* Translated from the Hawaiian by Nathaniel B. Emerson. Honolulu, HI: Bishop Museum Press.

Manzo, Kate. 1999. "Critical Humanism: Postcolonialism and Postmodern Ethics." Pp. 154–183 in *Moral Spaces* edited by David Campbell and Michael J. Shapiro. Minneapolis, MN: University of Minnesota Press.

Marshall, T. H. 1998 [1963]. "Citizenship and Social Class." Pp. 93–112 in *The Citizenship Debates* edited by Gershon Shafir. Minneapolis, MN: University of Minnesota Press.

Massey, Doreen. 1985. "New Directions in Space." Pp. 9–19 in *Social Relations and Spatial Structures* edited by Derek Gregory and John Urry. New York: St. Martin's Press.

Maunupau, Kamaki. 1994. "Ho'ohaole Maila 'Ia Kakou—Make Us into Whites." Pp. 44–48 in *Hawaii: Return to Nationhood.* Edited by Ulla Hasager and Jonathan Friedman. Copenhagen, Denmark: International Working Group for Indigenous Affairs.

Mayall, James. 1994 [1990]. "Irredentist and Secessionist Challenges." Pp. 269–280 in *Nationalism* edited by John Hutchinson and Anthony D. Smith. Oxford, UK: Oxford University Press.

McAdam, Doug. 1998. "The Future of Social Movements." Pp. 229–245 in *From Contention to Democracy* edited by Marco G. Giugni, Doug McAdam and Charles Tilly. Lanham, MD: Rowman and Littlefield.

McCarthy, John D. 1997. "The Globalization of Social Movement Theory." Pp. 243–259 in *Transnational Social Movements and Global Politics: Solidarity*

Beyond the State. Edited by Jackie Smith, Charles Chatfield, and Ron Pagnucco. Syracuse, NY: Syracuse University Press.

McGarry, John and Brendan O'Leary. 1996 [1993]. "Ethnic Conflict and Nationalism." Pp. 333–341 in *Ethnicity*, edited by John Hutchinson and Anthony D. Smith. Oxford, UK: Oxford University Press

Meller, Norman and Anne Feder Lee. 1997. "Hawaiian Sovereignty." Pp. 167–185 in *Publius: The Journal of Federalism*. 27:2.

Melucci, Alberto. 1995. "The Process of Collective Identity." Pp. 41–63 in *Social Movements and Culture* edited by Hank Johnston and Bert Klandermans. Minneapolis, MN: University of Minnesota Press.

"Mexico OKs Indian Rights Bill." 2001. *Global Exchange*. 13 June 2001. http://www.globalexchange.org/campaigns/mexico/news/ap071301.html (10 February 2003).

Minahan, James. 1996. *Nations Without States: A Historical Dictionary of Contemporary Nationalist Movements*. Westport, CT: Greenwood Press.

Minerbi, Luciano. 1994. "Native Hawaiian Struggles and Events: A Partial List 1973–1993." Pp. 1–14 in *Social Process in Hawai'i*. Volume 35.

———. 2001. "In the Face of Globalization: Two Decades of Insurgent Localism in Hawai'i." Pp. 165–189 in *Social Process in Hawai'i*. Volume 40.

Misztal, Barbara. 2000. *Informality: Social Theory and Contemporary Practice*. New York: Routledge.

Mitchell, Neil, Rhoda E. Howard, and Jack Donnelly. 1987. "Liberalism, Human Rights, and Human Dignity." Pp. 921–927 in *The American Political Science Review* 81:3.

Moore, F. W. 1968. "Current trends in cross-cultural research." Pp. 469–474 in *The Social Sciences: Problems and Orientations, Selected Studies*. The Hague, Netherlands: Mouton/UNESCO.

Mukerji, Chandra. 1983. *From Graven Images: Patterns of Modern Materialism*. New York: Columbia University Press.

———. 1997. *Territorial Ambitions and the Gardens of Versailles*. Cambridge, UK: Cambridge University Press.

Murphy, Alexander B. 1999. "International Law and the Sovereign State System: Challenges to the Status Quo" pp. 227–245 in *Reordering the World: Geopolitical Perspectives on the 21st Century* Second Edition. Edited by George J. Demko and William B. Wood. Boulder, CO: Westview Press.

Nash, Kate. 2000. *Readings in Contemporary Political Sociology*. Malden, MA: Blackwell Publishers.

Nagel, Joane. 1996. *American Indian Ethnic Renewal: Red Power and the Resurgence of Identity and Culture*. New York: Oxford University Press.

Nolan, Joseph R. and Jacqueline M. Nolan-Haley, with M. J. Connolly, Stephen C. Hicks, and Martina N. Alibrandi, contributing authors. 1990. *Black's Law Dictionary*. St. Paul, MN: West Publishing Co.

Omandam, Pat. 2002. "OHA Calls Ceded Lands Top Election Issue: Hawaiians will likely vote for those who support native rights." *Honolulu Star Bulletin*. 10 September 2002. http://starbulletin.com/2002/09/10/news/story4.html (11 September 2002).

Oommen, T. K. 1997. *Citizenship, Nationality and Ethnicity*. Cambridge, MA: Polity Press.
Osgood, Charles E. 1968. "On the strategy of cross-national research into subjective culture." Pp. 475–507 in *The Social Sciences: Problems and Orientations, Selected Studies*. The Hague, Netherlands: Mouton/UNESCO.
Osmani, S.R. 2000. "On Inequality." Pp. 143–160 in *The Blackwell Companion to Sociology* edited by Judith R. Blau. Cambridge, UK: Blackwell Publishers.
Osorio, Jonathan Kay Kamakawiwo'ole. 2002. Dismembering Lahui: A History of the Hawaiian Nation to 1887. Honolulu, HI: University of Hawai'i Press.
Paxman, John T. 1989. "Minority Indigenous Populations and Their Claims for Self-Determination." Pp. 185–202 in *Case Western Reserve Journal of International Law*. Volume 21.
Pieterse, Jan Nederveen. 2000. "Shaping Globalization." Pp. 1–19 in *Global Futures: Shaping Globalization*. Edited by Jan Nederveen Pieterse. London, UK: Zed Books.
Pitzer, Pat. 1998 [1984]. "Contemporary Kahuna." Pp. 293–306 in *Hawaii Chronicles II: Contemporary Island History*. Edited by Bob Dye. Honolulu, HI: University of Hawaii Press.
Premdas, Ralph R. 1998. "Secession and Decentralization: The Bougainville Case." Pp. 23–36 in *Canadian Review of Studies in Nationalism*, 25:1.
Price v. State of Hawaii. 764 F.2d 623 (9th Circuit 1985). Pp. 952–959 in *Federal Indian Law, Cases and Materials: Third Edition* edited by David H. Getches, Charles F. Wilkinson, and Robert A. Williams, Jr. St. Paul, MN: West Publishing Co.
Pocock, J. G. 1998 [1992]. "The Ideal of Citizenship since Classical Times." Pp. 31–42 in *The Citizenship Debates* edited by Gershon Shafir. Minneapolis, MN: University of Minnesota Press.
Poggi, Gianfranco. 1978. *The Development of the Modern State*. Stanford, CA: Stanford University Press.
Polletta, Francesca. 1998. "Contending Stories: Narrative in Social Movements." Pp. 419–456 in *Qualitative Sociology*, 21:4.
Popper, Karl. 1959. *The Logic of Scientific Discovery*. London, UK: Hutchinson.
Poppi, Cesare. 1997. "Wider Horizons with Larger Details: Subjectivity, ethnicity and globalization." Pp. 284–305 in *The Limits of Globalization: Cases and Arguments*. Edited by Alan Scott. London, UK: Routledge.
Prejean, Nakoa. 1994. "Kanaka Maoli and the United Nations." Pp. 276–285 in *Hawaii: Return to Nationhood*. Edited by Ulla Hasager and Jonathan Friedman. Copenhagen, Denmark: International Working Group for Indigenous Affairs.
Price, Marie D. 1999. "Nongovernmental Organizations on the Geopolitical Front Line" pp. 260–278 in *Reordering the World: Geopolitical Perspectives on the 21st Century* Second Edition. Edited by George J. Demko and William B. Wood. Boulder, CO: Westview Press.
Ragin, Charles C. 1987. *The Comparative Method*. Berkeley, CA: University of California Press.

———. 1992. "Introduction: Cases of "What is a case?"" Pp. 1–18 in *What is a Case? Exploring the Foundations of Social Inquiry* edited by Charles C. Ragin and Howard Saul Becker. Cambridge, UK: Cambridge University Press.
Ramet, Sabrina P. 1998. "Profit Motives in Secession." Pp. 26–29 in *Society*, 35:5.
Rawls, John. 1998 [1985]. "Justice as Fairness in the Liberal Polity." Pp. 53–74 in *The Citizenship Debates* edited by Gershon Shafir. Minneapolis, MN: University of Minnesota Press.
Renan, Ernest. 1994 [1882]. "Qu'est-ce qu'une nation?" Pp. 17–18 in *Nationalism* edited by John Hutchinson and Anthony D. Smith. Oxford, UK: Oxford University Press.
Robertson, Roland. 1992. *Globalization: Social Theory and Global Culture*. London, UK: Sage Publications.
———. 1997. "Social Theory, Cultural Relativity and the Problem of Globality." Pp. 69–90 in *Culture, Globalization and the World-System*, edited by Anthony D. King. Minneapolis, MN: University of Minnesota Press.
Rousseau, Jean-Jacques. 1968. *The Social Contract*. Translated and Introduced by Maurice Cranston. London, UK: Penguin Books.
Sandefur, Gary D., Ronald R. Rindfus, and Barney Cohen, editors. 1996. *Changing Numbers, Changing Needs: American Indian demography and public health*. Washington, D.C.: National Academy Press.
Sahlins, Marshall D. 1958. *Social Stratification in Polynesia*. Seattle, WA: University of Washington Press.
———. 1968. *Tribesmen*. Englewood Cliffs, NJ: Prentice-Hall, Inc.
Said, Edward W. 1979. *Orientalism*. New York: Vintage Books.
Savage, Mike. 2001. "Political Sociology" pp. 253–267 in *The Blackwell Companion to Sociology* edited by Judith R. Blau. Malden, MA: Blackwell Publishers Inc.
Scott, Alan. 1997. "Introduction: Globalization: social process or political rhetoric?" Pp. 1–22 in *The Limits of Globalization: Cases and Arguments*. Edited by Alan Scott. London, UK: Routledge.
Scott, James C. 1976. *The Moral Economy of the Peasant: Rebellion and Subsistence in Southeast Asia*. New Haven, CT: Yale University Press.
———. 1998. *Seeing Like a State*. New Haven, CT: Yale University Press.
Searle, John R. 1995. *The Construction of Social Reality*. New York: The Free Press.
Selznick, Philip. 1966. *TVA and the Grass Roots: A Study of Politics and Organization*. New York: Harper and Row.
Sen, Amartya. 1999. *Development as Freedom*. New York: Alfred A. Knopf.
Seton-Watson, Hugh. 1994 [1977]. "Old and New Nations." Pp. 134–137 in *Nationalism* edited by John Hutchinson and Anthony D. Smith. Oxford, UK: Oxford University Press.
Shafir, Gershon. 1998. Introduction. Pp. 1–28 in *The Citizenship Debates*. Edited by Gershon Shafir. Minneapolis, MN: University of Minnesota Press.
Shapiro, Michael J. 1999. "The Ethics of Encounter: Unreading, Unmapping the Imperium." Pp. 57–91 in *Moral Spaces* edited by David Campbell and Michael J. Shapiro. Minneapolis, MN: University of Minnesota Press.

"Significant Dates in the History of Hawaii." n.d. *The Hawaiian Historical Society.* http://www.hawaiianhistory.org/ref/chron.html (2 May 2001).

Sikkink, Kathryn. 2004. "Restructuring World Politics: The Limits and Asymmetries of Soft Power." Pp. 301–317 in *Restructuring World Politics: Transnational Social Movements, Networks, and Norms.* Edited by Sanjeev Khagram, James V. Riker, and Kathryn Sikkink. Minneapolis, MN: University of Minnesota Press.

Simmel, Georg. 1950. "The Stranger." Pp. 402–408 in *The Sociology of Georg Simmel*, translated, edited and with an introduction by Kurt H. Wolf. New York: The Free Press.

Skocpol, Theda. 1988. *States and Social Revolutions: A Comparative Analysis of France, Russia, and China.* Cambridge, UK: Cambridge University Press.

Sluyk, Robin. 1996. *Hawaii: Report of the UNPO Mission to Hawai'i, June 30-July9 1996.* Unrepresented Nations and Peoples Organization. www.unpo.org/Downloads/Hawaii%20Report%201996.doc (25 May 2006).

Smith, Anthony D. 1998. *Nationalism and Modernism.* New York: Routledge.

Snipp, C. Matthew. 1989. *American Indians: the first of this land.* New York: Russell Sage Foundation.

"Solomon survivors tell their story." 2003. *BBC News World Edition.* 4 January 2003. http://news.bbc.co.uk/2/hi/asia-pacific/2626743.stm (6 January 2003).

Spencer, Metta, editor. 1998. *Separatism: Democracy and Disintegration.* Lanham, MD: Rowman and Littlefield.

Spybey, Tony. 1996. *Globalization and World Society.* Oxford, UK: Polity Press.

Srebrnik, Henry. 2001. "Mini-Nationalism, Self-Determination and Micro-States in a Globalized World." Pp. 1–8 in *Canadian Review of Studies in Nationalism,* 28:1.

Stalin, Joseph. 1994 [1973]. "The Nation." Pp. 18–21 in *Nationalism* edited by John Hutchinson and Anthony D. Smith. Oxford, UK: Oxford University Press.

Stone, John. 1996 [1979]. "Internal Colonialism." Pp. 278–281 in *Ethnicity*, edited by John Hutchinson and Anthony D. Smith. Oxford, UK: Oxford University Press.

Tabb, William K. 2002. *Unequal Partners.* New York: The New Press.

Tarrow, Sydney. 2000 [1998]. "Transnational Contention." Pp. 177–202 in *Readings in Contemporary Political Sociology* edited by Kate Nash. Malden, MA: Blackwell Publishers.

Thomas, Daniel C. 2004. "Human Rights in U.S. Foreign Policy." Pp. 71–95 in *Restructuring World Politics: Transnational Social Movements, Networks, and Norms.* Edited by Sanjeev Khagram, James V. Riker, and Kathryn Sikkink. Minneapolis, MN: University of Minnesota Press.

Tilly, Charles. 1975. *The Formation of National States in Western Europe.* Princeton, NJ: Princeton University Press.

———. 1999. *Durable Inequality.* Berkeley, CA: University of California Press.

Trask, Haunani-Kay. 1994 [1992]. "Kupa'a 'Aina." Pp. 15–32 in *Hawaii: Return to Nationhood.* Edited by Ulla Hasager and Jonathan Friedman. Copenhagen, Denmark: International Working Group for Indigenous Affairs.

———. 1994 [1990]. "Politics in the Pacific Islands: Imperialism and Native Self-Determination." Pp. 259–275 in *Hawaii: Return to Nationhood*. Edited by Ulla Hasager and Jonathan Friedman. Copenhagen, Denmark: International Working Group for Indigenous Affairs.

———. 1999. *From a Native Daughter: Colonialism and Sovereignty in Hawai'i*. Honolulu, HI: University of Hawaii Press.

Trask, Mililani B. 1994. "The Politics of Oppression." Pp. 71–87 in *Hawaii: Return to Nationhood*. Edited by Ulla Hasager and Jonathan Friedman. Copenhagen, Denmark: International Working Group for Indigenous Affairs.

Tully, James. 1995. *Strange Multiplicity: Constitutionalism in an Age of Diversity*. Cambridge, UK: Cambridge University Press.

Turner, Jonathan. 1998. *The Structure of Sociological Theory*. Sixth Edition. Belmont, CA: Wadsworth Publishing Company.

Turpel, Mary Ellen. 1992. "Indigenous Peoples' Rights of Political Participation and Self-Determination: Recent International Legal Developments and the Continuing Struggle for Recognition." Pp. 579–602 in *Cornell International Law Journal*. Volume 23.

United Nations. 1945. *United Nations Charter, Chapter XI Declaration Regarding Non-Self-Governing Territories, Article 73*. Hawai'i Independent and Sovereign. http://www.hawaii-nation.org/art73.html (4 March 2003).

———. 1948. *Universal Declaration of Human Rights*. United Nations. http://www.un.org/Overview/rights.html (27 September 2002).

———. 1960. *Declaration on the Granting of Independence to Colonial Countries and Peoples*. General Assembly. Fifteenth Session. Resolution 1514. *Hawai'i Independent and Sovereign*. http://www.hawaii-nation.org/1514.html (4 March 2003). Also available online at *United Nations Documentation*. Pp. 66–67. http://ods-dds-ny.un.org/doc/RESOLUTION/GEN/NR0/152/88/IMG/NR015288.pdf?OpenElement (16 May 2003).

———. 1966. *International Covenant on Civil and Political Rights*. General Assembly. Twenty-first Session. Resolution 2200A. *Hawai'i Independent and Sovereign*. http://www.hawaii-nation.org/iccpr.html (4 March 2003). Also available online at *United Nations Documentation*. Pp. 52–60. http://ods-dds-ny.un.org/doc/RESOLUTION/GEN/NR0/005/03/IMG/NR000503.pdf?OpenElement (16 May 2003).

———. 1989. *Convention on the Rights of the Child*. Office of the United Nations High Commissioner for Human Rights. *Office of the High Commissioner for Human Rights*. http://www.unhchr.ch/html/menu3/b/k2crc.htm (4 April 2003).

———. 2001. Security Council. "Complaint Against the United States of America." Submitted by David Keanu Sai (agent). *Hawai'i Independent and Sovereign*. http://www.HawaiianKingdom.org/united-nations.shtml (22 February 2003)

———. 2002. Economic and Social Council. "Historic Permanent Forum on Indigenous Issues Breaks New Ground for World's Indigenous Peoples." Press Release HR/4588. *United Nations*. 5 October 2002. http://www.un.org/News/Press/docs/2002/hr4588.doc.htm (14 May 2002).

———. Working Group on Indigenous Populations. 1994. *UN Draft Declaration on the Rights of Indigenous Peoples*. As printed in *Indigenous Peoples in*

International Law by S. James Anaya. 1996. Oxford UK: Oxford University Press.

United Nations Educational, Scientific and Cultural Organization. 2001a. "Draft UNESCO Declaration on Cultural Diversity." *United Nations Educational, Scientific and Cultural Organization Documentary Resources*. 23 October 2001 http://unesdoc.unesco.org/images/0012/001234/123405e.pdf. (27 September 2002).

———. 2001b. "UNESCO Universal Declaration on Cultural Diversity." *United Nations Educational, Scientific and Cultural Organization*. 25 January 2002. http://www.unesco.org/culture/pluralism/diversity/html_eng/index_en.shtml (28 March 2003).

United States Congress. House. 1990. *Native American Graves Protection and Repatriation Act*. 101st Congress, H.R. 5237. *Hawai'i Independent and Sovereign*. http://www.hawaii-nation.org/nagpra.html (4 March 2003).

United States Congress. Senate. Subcommittee on Constitutional Rights. 1968. *Indian Civil Rights Act (ICRA)*. 25 USC 1301–1303. *Tribal Court Development: Alaska Tribes, Third Edition*. 2002. Lisa JaegerTribal Government Specialist for the Tanana Chiefs Conference,Inc. http://thorpe.ou.edu/AKtribalct/appendix_a.html (3 May 2003).

United States Congress. 1993. *United States Public Law 103–150*. 103d Congress Joint Resolution 19. *Hawai'i Independent and Sovereign*. http://www.hawaii-nation.org/publawall.html (5 May 2003).

United States Constitution. http://www.constitutioncenter.org/explore/TheU.S.Constitution/index.html#Amendments (27 September 2002).

Uprichard, Brett. 1998 [1988]. "Dr. Emmet Aluli Interview." Pp. 307–323 in *Hawaii Chronicles II: Contemporary Island History*. Edited by Bob Dye. Honolulu, HI: University of Hawaii Press.

Vitti, Vicki. 2002. "OHA submits ceded lands tab." *Honolulu Advertiser*. 1 November 2002. http://the.honoluluadvertiser.com/article/2002/Nov/01/br/br05p.hmtl (1 November 2002).

Wagner, Peter. 2001. "Modernity: One or Many?" pp. 30–42 in *The Blackwell Companion to Sociology* edited by Judith R. Blau. Malden, MA: Blackwell Publishers Inc.

Wallace, III., William Kauaiwiuloakalani. 1994. "La'ie: Land and People in Transition." Pp. 88–107 in *Social Process in Hawai'i*. Volume 36.

Wallerstein, Immanuel. 1997a. "The National and the Universal: Can There Be Such a Thing as World Culture?" Pp. 91–105 in *Culture, Globalization and the World-System*, edited by Anthony D. King. Minneapolis, MN: University of Minnesota Press.

———. 1997b. "States? Sovereignty? The Dilemmas of Capitalists in an Age of Transition." Keynote address at conference on "State and Sovereignty in the World Economy." University of California at Irvine. http://fbc.binghamton.edu/iwsovty.htm (6 April 2006).

———. 1999a. *The End of the World as We Know It*. Minneapolis, MN: University of Minnesota Press.

———. 1999b. "Globalization or The Age of Transition? A Long-Term View of the Trajectory of the World-System." *Binghamton University, State University* of New York. Fernand Braudel Center for the Study of Economies, Historical Systems, Civilizations. http://fbc.binghamton.edu/iwtrajws.htm (14 April 2003).

———. 2000. *The Essential Wallerstein*. New York: The New Press.

———. 2002. "New Revolts Against the System." Pp. 29–39 in *New Left Review* 18: Nov/Dec.

Warner, Daniel. 1999. "Searching for Responsibility/Community in International Relations." Pp. 1–28 in *Moral Spaces* edited by David Campbell and Michael J. Shapiro. Minneapolis, MN: University of Minnesota Press.

Weber, Max. 1946. *From Max Weber: Essays in Sociology*. Translated and edited by H. H. Gerth and C. Wright Mills. New York: Oxford University Press.

———. 1994 [1946]. "The Nation." Pp. 21–25 in *Nationalism* edited by John Hutchinson and Anthony D. Smith. Oxford, UK: Oxford University Press.

———. 1978. *Economy and Society, Parts One and Two*. Edited by Guenther Roth and Claus Wittich. Berkeley, CA: University of California Press.

———. 1998 [1981]. "Citizenship in Ancient and Medieval Cities." Pp. 43–49 in *The Citizenship Debates* edited by Gershon Shafir. Minneapolis, MN: University of Minnesota Press.

Whitney, Scott. 1998 [1994]. "Capturing the Ka'ai." Pp. 348–365 in *Hawaii Chronicles II: Contemporary Island History*. Edited by Bob Dye. Honolulu, HI: University of Hawaii Press.

Wilkins, Burleigh T. 2000. "Secession." Pp. 15–22 in *Peace Review*, 12:1.

Wilmer, Franke. 1997 [1993]. "First nations in the USA." Pp. 186–201 in *The Ethnicity Reader: Nationalism, Multiculturalism, and Migration*. Edited by Montserrat Guibernau and John Rex. Cambridge, UK: Polity Press.

Wolff, Janet. 1997. "The Global and the Specific: Reconciling Conflicting Theories of Culture." Pp. 161-173 in *Culture, Globalization and the World-System*, edited by Anthony D. King. Minneapolis, MN: University of Minnesota Press.

Wood, Houston. 1999. *Displacing Natives: The Rhetorical Production of Hawai'i*. Lanham, MD: Rowman and Littlefield Publishers, Inc.

Yamamoto, Eric K. and Chris Iijima. 2000. "The Colonizer's Story: The Supreme Court Violates Native Hawaiian Sovereignty—Again." *Color Lines*, 3:2. http://www.arc.org/C_Lines/CLArchive/story3_2_01.html (2 May 2001).

Young, Robert. 1995. *Colonial Desire: Hybridity in Theory, Culture, and Race*. London, UK: Routledge.

Young, Iris Marion. 1998 [1989]. *Polity and Group Difference: A Critique of the Ideal of Universal Citizenship*. Pp. 263–290 in *The Citizenship Debates*. Edited by Gershon Shafir. Minneapolis, MN: University of Minnesota Press.

Yurick, Sol. 1995. "The Emerging Metastate versus the Politics of Ethno-nationalist Identity." Pp. 204–224 in *The Decolonization of Imagination: Culture, Knowledge and Power* edited by Jan Nederveen Pieterse and Bhikhu Parekh. London: Zed Books Ltd.

Zapf, W. 1968. "Complex societies and social change: Problems of macrosociology." Pp. 252–265 in *The Social Sciences: Problems and Orientations, Selected Studies*. The Hague, Netherlands: Mouton/UNESCO.

Index

A
Aboriginal inhabitants of Hawaii, 27–28
Agard, Keoni Kealoha, 30, 45, 49–52, 55–57, 60–63
Aluli, Noa Emmett, 53
Amendments to U.S. Constitution, 109–110
American Indians, Native Hawaiians, contrasted, 4–7
Anaya, S. James, 4, 33, 86–88, 91
Ancestral roots
  in land, 27
Ancestry, sharing of, 27
Anderson, Benedict, 15, 69
Appadurai, Arjun, 3, 14, 70–72
Aristotle, 11
Autonomous communities, tradition-based, 28

B
Bauman, Zygmunt, 70, 73
Beck, Ulrich, 3, 71
Benhabib, Seyla, 99
Bennett, 99
Bhabha, Homi K., 73–74
Bill of Rights, U.S. Constitution, 109–110
Blaisdell, Kekuni, 48, 53, 58
Borland, Elizabeth, 42
Brown Thompson, Karen, 8

C
Calhoun, Craig, 7–8
Canby, Jr., William C., 5
Case studies, 26–30, 74–79
Castanha, Anthony, 58, 60–63
Cheru, Fantu, 70–71
Clifford, James, 33

Cohen, Bernard P., 19, 22
Colonies, experience as, 27, 29–30, 68–69
Commons, John R., 64
Concept, indigenous, 3–4
Connor, Walker, 12
Constitution of State of Hawaii, Article XII, 117–118
Constitutional Amendments, United States, 109–110
Cooper, David E. K., 104
Cornell, Stephen E., 19
Corntassel, Jeff J., 88
Creole hybrid, 69
Cultural traditions, life in conformity with, 30
Culturally distinct community, 38
Customs, life in conformity with, 30

D
Data gathering, 25–26
Day, A. Grove, 46–48
Definition of indigenousness, 33–34
Deloria, Jr. Vine, 5, 7
Description of project, 99–100
Deutsch, Karl W., 12
Donnelly, Jack, 16, 83, 104
DuBois, W. E. B., 73, 81, 100
Dudley, Michael Kioni, 30, 45, 49–52, 55–57, 60–63

E
Economic impact, sovereign Hawaii, 54–55
Economic traditions, life in conformity with, 30
Eriksen, Thomas Hylland, 33
Evans, Peter B., 12

Experience as colonies, 27, 29–30, 68–69

F
Falk, Richard, 71
Field-Grace, Sondra, 61–62
Finnemore, Martha, 8
First generation human rights, 84–85
Fleras, Augie, 40
Friedman, Thomas L., 43

G
Gandhi, Leela, 73, 81, 100
Getches, David H., 5, 45, 47, 51–52, 60
Giddens, Anthony, 11–12, 69, 71–72, 79, 105
Gilroy, Paul, 73–74
Global identity, 72
 examples of, 75–76
Globalization, 69–71
Gomes, L. Ku'umeaaloha, 47
Greider, William, 71
Griffin, Keith, 70
Guibernau, Montserrat, 4, 10, 33, 43
Gutmann, Amy, 84, 91

H
Hall, Stuart, 2–3, 70, 72
Hartwell, Jay, 28, 52, 59, 76–77, 79
Hawaiian Affairs, Hawaiian Homes Commission Act
 Acceptance of Compact, 117
 Traditional/Customary Rights, 117
Hayden, Tom, 94
Hechter, Michael, 42
Heckathorn, 52, 57–60
Hobbes, Thomas, 11–12
Hoppe, Hans-Hermann, 13
Howard, Rhoda E., 16, 83, 88, 104
Human rights, 83–97
 first generation human rights, 84–85
 freedoms sought, 89–90
 indigenous rights, as human rights, 87–89
 native Hawaiians, 90–92
 relational concept, 103
 second generation human rights, 85–86
 third generation human rights, 86–87
 Universal Declaration of Human Rights, protections under, 93–95
 in world-systems theory, 16–17
 Zapatistas, 92–93
Hybridity, 73–74
 examples of, 78–79

I
Identity, relational concept, 102
Identity types, 72–74
 case studies, 74–79
 global identity, 72
 examples of, 75–76
 hybridity, 73–74
 examples of, 78–79
 local identity, 72–73
 examples of, 76–78
Ignatieff, Michael, 16
Independent Hawaii, 45–66
 economic impact, 54–55
 land, 51–54
 for native Hawaiians, 53
 for United States, 53–54
 renaissance to present, 55–60
 renaissance to present day, 55–60
 sovereignty, 64–65
 sovereignty movement organizations, 60–64
Indian Civil Rights Act of 1968, 119–120
Indians, American, Native Hawaiians, contrasted, 4–7
Indigenous rights, as human rights, 87–89
Institutional state structure, traditional customs, contrasted, 30
Interactions with state, 79–81
Internal colony experience, 68–69
Ito, Karen L., 78–79

K
Kellner, Douglas, 70
Kelly, John, 57
Khagram, Sanjeev, 8
Kohler, Gernot, 71
Krasner, Stephen D, 13, 64
Kuykendall, Ralph S., 46–48
Kymlicka, Will, 3, 87, 89

L
Lam, Maivan Clech, 88
Land, 51–54
Land significance
 native Hawaiians, 53
 United States, 53–54
Lands, ancestral roots in, 27
Legitimacy of indigenousness, 41–43
Levi, Margaret, 11–12
Livingston, Donald W, 13

Index

Lo, Ming-cheng M., 74, 81
Local identity, 72–73
    examples of, 76–78
Local traditions, maintenance of, 29

M

Maaka, Roger, 40
Maiguashca, Bice, 89
Malo, David, 46
Massey, Doreen, 68
Maunupau, Kamaki, 47–48, 56
McGregor, Davianna Pomaika'I, 53
Methodology, 24–25
Minahan, James, 45, 47, 51
Mitchell, Neil, 16, 83, 104
Mokuau, Noreen, 48, 53, 58
Mukerji, Chandra, 14–15

N

Nash, Kate, 7, 12
Nation
    state, relation between, 12–14
    in world-systems theory, 9–11
Nation-state, in world-systems theory, 12
National characteristics of predominant population *vs.* traditional, 30

O

Oommen, T. K., 11–12, 16, 71
Organizations of sovereignty movement, 60–64
Outside society, incorporation of elements, 29

P

Pitzer, Pat, 48
Poggi, Gianfranco, 14, 68
Political movement, 7–9
Popper, Karl, 21
Predominant customs, traditional customs, contrasted, 30
Primeau, Tomas Hopkins, 88
Problematizing indigenousness, 34–38
Project description, 99–100

R

Ragin, Charles C., 24
Relational concept
    human rights, 103
    identity, 102
    indigenousness as, 38–41

Renaissance, Hawaiian, through present, 55–60
Research design, 21–31
    1 theory, 21–24
    case study, 26–30
    data gathering, 25–26
    methodology, 24–25
Riker, James V., 8
Rindfus, Ronald R., 19
Robertson, Roland, 3, 70, 74
Roots, ancestral, in lands, 27
Rousseau, Jean-Jacques, 11
Rueschemeyer, Dietrich, 12

S

Sahlins, Marshall D., 46–47, 51, 54–55
Sandefur, Gary D., 19
Second generation human rights, 85–86
Sharing of ancestry, 27
Sikkink, Kathryn, 8
Skocpol, Theda, 12
Sluyk, Robin, 1
Snipp, C. Matthew, 19
Social characteristics of predominant population *vs.* traditional, 30
Social customs, life in conformity with, 30
Sovereign Hawaii, 45–66
    economic impact, 54–55
    land, 51–54
        for native Hawaiians, 53
        for United States, 53–54
    organizations of sovereignty movement, 60–64
    renaissance, through present, 55–60
Spybey, Tony, 69–72
State
    interaction with, identity and, 79–81
    nation, relation between, in world-systems theory, 12–14
    in world-systems theory, 11–12
State structure, traditional customs, contrasted, 30
Stone, John, 68

T

Tabb, William K., 71
Territory, in world-systems theory, 14–16
Third generation human rights, 86–87
Tradition-based autonomous communities, 28
Traditions
    life in conformity with, 30

maintenance of, 29
Trask
    Haunani-Kay, 14–15, 34, 45, 47–53, 56–64, 66, 75, 87, 89, 91, 93
    Mililani B., 53, 60
Tully, James, 11–12
Turner, Jonathan, 21
Types of identities, 72–74
    global, 72
    hybridity, 73–74
    local, 72–73
Types of identity, 72–74
    case studies, 74–79
    global identity, 72
        examples of, 75–76
    hybridity, 73–74
        examples of, 78–79
    local identity, 72–73
        examples of, 76–78

U
United States Public Law 103–150, 111–116
Universal Declaration of Human Rights, 93–95, 121–122

Uprichard, Brett, 51, 53

W
Wagner, Peter, 72
Wallerstein, Immanuel, 9, 11, 21, 40, 80–81
Weber, Max, 10–12
Wilkins, David E., 5, 7
Wilkinson, Charles F., 45, 47, 51, 60
Williams, Robert A., Jr., 5, 45, 47, 51–52, 60
Wilmer, Franke, 40
World-systems theory, 9
    nation, 9–11
    nation-state, 12
    state, 11–12
        nation, relation between, 12–14

Y
Young, Iris Marion, 91

Z
Zapatistas, 92–93
Zapf, W., 22